SERVING HEROES

Dr. B. Sky

ISBN 979-8-88616-370-4 (paperback)
ISBN 979-8-88616-372-8 (hardcover)
ISBN 979-8-88616-371-1 (digital)

Christian Faith Publishing
832 Park Avenue
Meadville, PA 16335
www.christianfaithpublishing.com

Printed in the United States of America

To all the veterans who served to keep America
safe and free. God bless America!

CONTENTS

PREFACE

This is my third book, and the timeframe I write about occurs prior to the timeframe of my first two books, true stories, *Oh, the Things They Like to Hide* and *Slaying the Giant, Uncovering the Things They Like to Hide*. These two books expose true facts about politicians, a large health-care system, coercion, and how unsolicited political pressure placed upon physicians and providers can thwart efforts to apply opioid safety initiatives in America leading to unintentional drug overdoses. You do not have to read *Oh, the Things They Like to Hide* or *Slaying the Giant, Uncovering the Things They Like to Hide* first; however, I do highly recommend reading the books at some point. I pray you enjoy this book, *Serving Heroes*, also a true story about men and women who valiantly served our country.

I battled opioid safety for patients for fifteen years at a large health-care organization to save lives of patients and citizens in the community. When a politician and medical center director entered into the picture with selfish ambitions, they illegally practiced medicine through coercion, threats, and blame. They chose to be blind to the fact that people were overdosing on prescription opioid medications, and they chose patient and voter satisfaction over saving lives. The duo ignored truth and embraced self-interest along with selfish ambition. The director and politician threatened clinicians in opposition, using a weak chief of staff as a pawn to potentially take the heat off of their political agendas. Their narcissistic goals collided with patient care. Their greedy pursuits resulted in destruction. The destruction each created ended careers for altruistic health-care providers and leaders, created a hostile work environment for remaining employees, resulted in a shortage of physicians to care for patients, and worse yet, led to loss of life for patients at the facility and in the community. My story about my experiences at Veterans Health Administration (VA) ended badly. The beginning of my story started out challenging; but I cared for the greatest generation of veterans which proved to be a high honor.

ACKNOWLEDGMENTS

First, to God be the glory!

Secondly, thank you to my dear husband, Mark. Thank you for bringing out the good in me. Thank you for spoiling me and blessing my life. Most of all, thank you for showing the kind of love that Jesus wants us all to show to others.

My gratitude extends beyond what can be expressed in writing. God blessed me by providing me an opportunity to serve veterans for eighteen years. He blessed me to work alongside wonderful nursing staff, colleagues, medical support staff, clerical staff, and volunteers. Our mission: to serve veterans.

Thank you to organizations supporting our veterans. Thank you to organizers of community events that celebrate veterans. Thank you to all of the volunteers serving our veterans.

Thank you, most holy and wonderful God, for guiding our country. May we turn from our wicked ways and acknowledge our need for a God-led United States of America.

> If My people, who are called by My name, shall humble themselves and pray, and seek My face and turn from their wicked ways, then will I hear from heaven, and will forgive their sin and will heal their land. (2 Chronicles 7:14, KJV)

INTRODUCTION

I attended medical school at the age of thirty, a time when everyone thought this was too old to pursue such a lofty career. I defied the allopathic (MD) schools after multiple rejections due to my age and other political influences at that time, which pales to my current story so we will skip that part of my life. University of Health Sciences College of Osteopathic Medicine in Kansas City, Missouri, welcomed me with open arms during my interview visit. Four years later, I graduated third in my class which began with 171 students.

The road to becoming a doctor started in Kansas City. It was the first time I went to school outside of the Cleveland, Ohio, area. I was thrilled to experience the change in location. I had been to every school in the Cleveland area previously: Cuyahoga Community College, Baldwin Wallace College, Cleveland State University, and Case Western University School of Dentistry.

I attended University of Health Sciences College of Osteopathic Medicine. It was a great school for me. Somehow, I seemed to fit there, and I did well.

Finances were always a burden for me. I worked as a dental hygienist to put myself through undergraduate school. By the time I made it to medical school, I was deep into debt. I couldn't work in medical school due to the heavy workload, so I thought, *Now what?*

I looked into military options for the third time in my life. I almost joined the United States Army after high school, but I chickened out. Later, I seriously checked out the United States Air Force; but I never finished the process. This was my last chance to join the military due to my age; but it turned out to be the best. I received acceptance into the Naval Health Professions Scholarship Program (HPSP). Essentially, the military paid my entire tuition, books, related equipment, and gave me a stipend to live on (almost) each month. The kicker was that I was sworn in during the heat of Desert Storm (Jan 17, 1991–February 28,1991) on February 12, 1991. My mom cried.

Ensign "With Distinction" Lori Drumm, Officer Indoctrination School, Newport, Rhode Island July 26, 1991

Medical school became unbearable for me by the second year. I was drowning in books and stress. It's funny, but the Lord always knows what He is doing. Because I was now connected to the military, when those times came that I wanted to quit, I hung in there. You see, if I quit medical school, I would still have to serve in the Navy. This kept me from quitting, even though it felt like I was hanging by a fine golden thread.

I obviously survived medical school. Then came the worst year of my life at that point in time, internship year. It was a year of incredible growth, along with incredible pain. I spent the year never feeling rested. I ended up with post-traumatic stress disorder related to beepers/pagers. I presently cannot wear a pager or anything that beeps. I tolerate my cell phone now thankfully. The major lesson learned during my internship was, never make major decisions post on call or during times of sleep deprivation. I was post on call, up all night in the intensive care unit (ICU). I had had it. I was beaten up royally during morning report by insensitive, arrogant attending physicians who loved beefing up their egos by tearing down inexperienced medical interns. I decided to quit the internship program; but luckily for me, the internship program director was not in the office that morning. I headed home to sleep and came back to the hospital feeling totally different about the situation. Thank you, Jesus!

I learned a serious lesson involving the hazard of post on call. As a passenger riding with a post on call driver on a winding road, he suddenly started reading x-rays aloud. You see, he was asleep, dreaming, and driving the car! I screamed, and he woke up. We did not crash, praise God! But my friend from medical school did. He fell asleep, crossed the midline of the road, and killed a newlywed couple along with himself. Tragic!

During medical school, many people supported me. I went home to Ohio as much as I could. I missed my mom and my friends. These were my best friends.

Merle Fuss, Jenni Jallos Sammon, Lori Drumm, Kim Eckhardt Cuebas

Whenever I came to town, they dropped everything, and we got together. I looked forward to finishing each set of midterm and final examinations with visits home whenever possible. My friends never forgot about me. Funny, for some time, I ended up living back in the Cleveland area, although I rarely saw them due to the busyness of life. But they were there for me when I needed them and they are forever in my heart. We manage to visit when time allows, and we pick right up where we left off. I cherish these friends along with new friendships made through life's journey.

Time came to serve as an active-duty general medical officer (GMO) for the military. By the grace of God, the Navy stationed me at Groton Connecticut Submarine Base on the East Coast. I lived in Mystic, Connecticut, as if part of a beautiful fairy tale. My backyard abutted a river filled with tall ships and a hillside of beautiful homes and trees that looked like someone painted their fantasy. I could put on my rollerblades and skate down the prettiest river road along-side beautiful landscapes and majestic homes with big white pillars. I received amazing training during my military service. I completed certification in advance trauma life support (ATLS). I completed combat casualty care course (C4) at Camp Bullis Military Training Reservation, a US Army training camp expanding 27,990 acres in Bexar County, Texas; multivictim child sexual abuse and family advocacy staff training at various locations, and fleet hospital training at Navy Fleet Hospital Operational Training Command, Camp Pendleton, California. I learned how to rappel down towers, cross rivers on ropes, and drag a bag of sand, my patient, through water under wire while being shot at by the enemy, all the while smiling for the camera because it was all simulated.

Combat casualty care course, Camp Bullis, Texas

Simulation exercise, Camp Pendleton, California, September 20, 1996

The military training was great. During fleet hospital training, I learned how to build a hospital from the ground up. Then once built, I experienced the role of triage officer and how to survive combat in addition to surviving constipation from eating MREs (meals ready to eat). I wasn't always the doctor. I was also a patient, sick as can be; but I got better and had a blast dancing by the end of training.

On the downside, I learned about failed relationships through my military medical career. I married a man that could not accept my commitment to the military. He and his family failed to understand a person cannot "quit the military," so he quit the marriage. Since I was assigned to a command in a different state, I couldn't leave to try to make the marriage work. It was a rough lesson to learn. I felt helpless because I couldn't quit my job as an officer that raised her hand to support our country no matter the cost. I paid with my marriage; but many people paid with their lives. Ultimately, I healed, and I now accept that I did not have a choice in the matter. It is well with my soul.

On the brighter side, one of my best friends from medical school, Dennis, raised his right hand in service to our country at about the same time I raised my right hand. The Lord was again at work. Dennis and I landed in Newport, Rhode Island, assigned to the same company, Kilo Company, during Officer Indoctrination School (OIS). How comforting! This inspiring, hilarious Christian friend added inspiration and humor to grueling training and endless days of buffing floors, cleaning window sills with cotton tips, polishing shoes, marching for hours, studying for tests, training for the service life, and enduring many inspections. Dennis and his wife, Stefanie, survived medical school, their military commitment, and they are enjoying each other and their five children to this day.

Other medical school friends also did very well in their relationships. They went on to marry and have families during and after medical school, internships, and residencies. It can be done! My closest friend, Sherie, gave birth to her first child while in medical school. I coached her during the delivery until her husband arrived from California, and we rejoiced at the birth of Ryan. Time flew by as it always does, and Ryan graduated from our same medical school and presently serves as a Navy physician. What blessings God gives us along life's journey. I see God's hand in my life, especially as I look back in time.

I finished my active-duty obligation, and I decided to open a solo general practice in Rhode Island. This was not an easy decision to make, and I will spare you the details. After a lot of sweat, hard work, and planning, the practice opened.

Cheryl Volk, RN, Navy veteran, and Lori Drumm, DO, Navy veteran

A medical equipment representative befriended me when I practiced medicine as a community physician. He ended up stalking me later on, much to my surprise. I had to call the police and then his boss to report him when he finally crossed the line and threatened me during office hours in front of patients. He initially was a friendly representative who became a surprising threat. I was totally fooled.

Then there's Stacy (not her real name) with the "girl next door" appearance of sweetness, huge smile, unending charm; and her big hiring asset was she attended my church regularly. Lesson learned: Don't ever hire church members, friends, or family without fully checking backgrounds. Who would ever think that a smiling angel-ic-appearing employee would put me through tremendous trials and tribulation? By the time I figured out her agenda and activities, I had been taken advantage of financially, and Lord only knows for how long. Once I had proof of her activities, I fired her and subsequently suffered for months. She changed all of the passwords on my accounts, sent a letter to the Occupational Safety and Health

Administration (OSHA), stating I did not use gloves in the office. I believe she and the stalker stole multiple items from my home and office. She used the office computer and telephone for personal use, and at that time, phone companies billed for professional telephone calls and computer time. I constantly wondered what kind of stunt she would pull next, which made sleeping difficult. I later learned that she had been fired from a well-known company for blackmail and participated in shady activities. Another medical office just a block away hired Stacy, and I expect she went on to rob and torment her next boss. I learned not all churchgoers are Christians.

I hired a former Navy corpsman. She proved to be organized, trustworthy, and reliable; but I wondered about her attitude. She rarely smiled. I wondered about her relationship with our patients, even though I never heard anyone complain. At a performance review, I expressed my concern, but she did not have much to say in return. Her other qualities weighed heavily in favor of continuing her employment, and I invested in medical insurance for both of us as full-time employees. Later, what I thought was an attitude concern turned out to be extreme illness. Once Alice (not her real name) visibly declined due to illness, I admitted her with the diagnosis of severe malnutrition due to active Crohn's disease, an intestinal inflammatory disease. I treated Alice during her month-long hospital stay. Alice ended up being one of my best employees and a good friend. I spent the rest of my days in private practice trying to make it up to her. We spent holidays together, enjoyed frequent dinners, including a lobster tall ship festival out at sea, visits to see my dad in Connecticut for special parties, and we baked cookies together. We kept in contact for years. She returned to Florida where her family still lived, gave birth to a beautiful baby girl, and began a medical career down south.

I survived private practice by the grace of God and great friends. I stayed out East due to my church family at the time. My closest friends from my Navy life and I attended church together. They were my lifeline back then as Christian friends. We were very close, and we did everything together. We shopped together, played volleyball together, ate meals together, celebrated holidays and weddings together, crafted together, cruised together, and more. I watched my friends' kids when a group from church went on a cruise in September of 2001. When the planes hit the twin towers on September 11, 2001, I was working in my office when a friend burst through the door, yelling for me to look at the news on television. We could not believe our eyes. We stared at the television in disbelief trying to comprehend the reality of the images flashing before our eyes. What would happen next? Did this act of terrorism mean war?

I remember packing my sea bags in preparation to be called to active duty for preparation for war. I was still on inactive duty status in the United States Naval Reserve (USNR). In the days which followed, I called the local recruiter and volunteered to be put into active status. I filled out the required paperwork to change my status. I wanted to actively serve again. The act of terrorism sparked my interest to defend my country.

During this same timeframe, I cared for my church friends' two girls. The cruise lines along with the rest of the country were in turmoil. Travel instantly became dangerous. Planes were grounded. Rental cars sold out. Many of my church friends became stuck in Florida, unable to return to their children and family members at a time where the country tied up telephone communication trying to ensure the status of their loved ones. Some of my friends secured a rental car and drove up from the cruise line docking station to Connecticut and Rhode Island. Others waited in endless lines trying to book a flight back home. Airline travel instantly became frightening. We lost trust in our ways of living. We lost trust in our homeland security. We grieved for those affected by the terrorists' acts on American soil. Just as we were all glued to the television craving information about the COVID-19 pandemic, we became thirsty for information. We searched for hope in the days to come and in the future for our children. Many turned and returned to God and faith in Jesus Christ after September 11, 2001. Church attendance rose across the nation. People began to seek comfort through our Lord, Jesus Christ. My book group friend, the one who came to my office that day, began seeking answers about Christ, and we talked extensively in those days. I thanked God for allowing me to be there for her during that difficult time of our lives.

I recall reaching out to my brother and my dad on that tragic day in history. They both traveled the world at that time, and I grew concerned about their location in the world on 9/11 and in the days to follow. Fortunately, they were safe and minimally affected by the travel restrictions. Interestingly, my dad was with his boss and boss's wife in Russia. My brother still travels around the world as a dental salesman, although a new tragedy, the COVID-19 pandemic, grounded him from travel until very recently. Gratefully, his company changed their way of doing business and adjusted their sales approach using video-based computer technology to carry out business transactions.

I was still attached to the awful beeper in private practice on the East Coast after 9/11 and slowly going crazy. Depression began to envelope me. I was sinking deeper into despair. I was isolated as a solo practitioner in a small town run by men—or so it seemed. Professionally, I was an outcast. What made the other professionals in town even more vindictive was that my practice grew, and I became successful from a worldly point of view. However, spiritually and emotionally, I was bankrupt.

One day, after Christmas in 2001, I decided to leave town to visit home in Ohio. I found someone to watch my practice. I ended up job hunting while home, and I ended up being hired by the Louis Stokes VA Medical Center practically on the spot. God answered my prayers. I knew I had to get home to the Midwest. I just did not know how to do it; but God knew. Five months later, I was heading home.

The Veterans Health Administration (VHA/VA) began as a good place for me to work as an outpatient physician. I lost my beeper a long time ago, but the issue of requiring physicians to wear beepers tended to pop up now and again. I really prayed I would not be forced to carry one of those evil things. Thankfully, beepers were replaced by smart phones. I enjoyed the patients and activities associated with working at the VA.

The VA hired me to work in a large clinic near the Canton Pro Football Hall of Fame and another clinic farther south in New Philadelphia. I commuted over an hour each way for a while from my mom's house on the west side of Cleveland; but I did not mind the long drive initially because I was grateful for the change in my career. To not be obligated to take twenty-four-hour on call thrilled me. What a relief!

I met Mark during a visit home in 2001. He saw my medical school graduation photograph on my mother's desk at work, and he admits he made up excuses to ask my mom about it. He still admits it and smiles to this day. If you knew my mom, she was very easy to speak with, and she would give you more information than you would ever want to know. All you needed to do is ask the question. Eight months later, Mark and I happily married and moved closer to my job near one of my favorite aunts. We actually bought her best friend's house, along with most of her furniture. I fondly remembered heading to Aunt Alice's house with high school friends to canoe and swim in the lake. I learned to drive there too. I smile in remembrance.

I enjoyed my new job immensely. To care for this special population of people, veterans, warmed my heart. Because I too belonged to this group, the patients accepted me openheartedly. They thought it was special to have their doctor be part of the comradery.

As a physician, I educated patients in hopes to change behavior that threatened their health, and I encouraged them to continue behavior that promoted good health. My nurses told me that I should teach. They said I was inspirational and informative. They said I was approachable, and they could tell that I enjoyed teaching. I served patients as part of a cohesive team that respected one another. My mood that I brought with me from the East Coast improved quickly after moving back home to the Midwest.

Reaching performance goals inspired me to continue efforts toward helping my patients take care of themselves physically, mentally, and spiritually. Because life had not been easy for me, I found myself able to empathize with many of the patients. I understood illness. I understood tragedy. I knew what it took to overcome the unfairness life can bring. By faith, I know that the Lord can, as the Christian speaker, Joyce Meyers, would say, "bring beauty out of ashes." I believed I communicated well with patients, and I invested of myself. I knew this because I was physically and emotionally exhausted at the end of the day; but it was worth the effort. I did not stop caring about the patients.

CHAPTER 1

LEGAL BATTLE
BOARD RULING

For those of you who read my first two books, *Oh, the Things They Like to Hide* and *Slaying the Giant, Uncovering the Things They Like to Hide*, this chapter discusses the outcome of my days in court. If this is your first book, I will give you a brief synopsis. I wrote *Serving Heroes* to shine a heavenly light as to why I stayed so long at the VA when, at times, the bad outweighed the good and the darkness overshadowed the light. I stayed to support the staff. We stayed to serve heroes.

The large health-care system is not a popular health-care organization in the eyes of the media and politicians. Political and media scrutiny abounds often resulting in defamation of character of dedicated employees working against enormous obstacles to improve patient health care. Subsequently, instead of supporting the medical staff, facility leaders choose to place undeserved blame on unsuspecting employees in a retaliatory approach. I became one of those unsuspecting employees when I tried to apply opioid safety initiatives as part of a nation-wide effort to save patients from unintentional overdose and death. I became a scapegoat. I became a whistleblower.

The agency employs many dedicated employees modeling the institution's core values of integrity, commitment, advocacy, and respect. Other employees wear the values on their coat pockets but fail to incorporate the admirable values into their hearts. Unfortunately, these other employees often occupy positions of power and deflect fatalist publicity on unsuspecting innocent targets. Following the shocking realization that the facility's executives blamed me for undesirable media and political inquiries, I knew I could not support the institution. The condemnation, finger-pointing, and retaliatory scrutiny became insurmountable. Worst of all, the crippling falsified accusations and distressing attention left me defenseless to protect patients within the institution and beyond.

My story uncovers the things they (disreputable leaders, politicians, and media personnel) like to hide about scandalous maneuvers by people in positions of power to deflect blame onto others when they face unsolicited investigations which would end careers and reflect poorly on the agency. My first two books described my response to becoming a scapegoat for the large health-care system, how I fought back to tell my side of the story, the truth as I know it, and the tedious process of preparing for court, my testimony and the testimonies by others, my brilliant attorneys' performances, and the aftermath of a whistleblowing process that took years to unfold.

True names and locations in the following have been redacted:

United States of America
Legal Battle Board

BAILEY B. SKY, Appellant
DOCKET NUMBER XR-1335
V.
LARGE HEALTHCARE SYSTEM, Agency

BEFORE
Administrative Judge
Initial Decision
Introduction

In the new year of 2018, Dr. B. Sky (appellant) filed an individual right of action alleging

the Large Healthcare System took various personnel actions in retaliation for her protected
whistleblowing activity. A hearing took place in
the spring of 2018.

I GRANT corrective action in part, and I
DENY corrective actions in part for reasons dis-
cussed below.

The judge outlined his analysis and findings. He began with
detailing my employment with the large health-care system. I began
employment at the Great Lakes Medical Center in 2002 as a primary care provider and later a clinical manager for eight years. I then
accepted an offer as the Primary and Specialty Care Service Line
Manager at Facility in the Land of Corn and Soybeans. I oversaw
pain management for the facility.

In the fall of 2015, the facility by the river health-care system
(FBTRHCS) appointed me as associate chief of staff of primary care.
I held that position for two years before retiring.

I was hired into this position at FBTRHCS following recruit-
ment based on my extensive pain management, opioid safety, and primary care management experiences. Appointed a first-line supervisor
of primary care physicians, some located in rural sites, I performed
a number of duties including running a primary care department,
clinical reviews, quality reviews, credentialing and privileging duties,
application of opioid safety initiatives sent down from headquarters,
and keeping senior executives informed regularly of department and
task force accomplishments. My first-line supervisor was Dr. Chief
of Staff, and my second line supervisor was Mr. Director. Dr. Chief
of Staff rated my performance as outstanding for the rating period of
fiscal year 2016.

As opioid safety prescribing champion, clinicians often sought
my guidance regarding pain management. Primary care providers
prescribed opioids for chronic pain. A pain management prescriber
was to be appointed for assistance, but this had not occurred, which
meant all of the prescribing landed on the primary care providers'

shoulders in addition to many other duties. "All roads lead to primary care" was the facility's motto. Basically, primary care providers were burdened with their own primary care tasks, much of specialty medicines duties pertaining to prescriptions and test orders, application of opioid safety initiatives, and coordinating care for the patient in the community in addition to the facility.

The judge stated that I served as the interface between frontline prescribers and executives. He stated my testimony was credible regarding my "extensive experience, training, and certifications in the area of pain management and opioid prescription practices."

During my stay at FBTRHCS, I raised concerns to leaders about opioid prescription practices and concerns about the amounts of opioids being prescribed by the providers. I outlined why these practices were a concern in relation to health risks, including but not limited to unintentional overdoses and death (which had occurred).

Under my leadership and in line with the opioid safety initiative task force goals from headquarters, primary care providers began tapering and suspending opioid prescription as appropriate. Pain agreements, urine drug screens, pill counts, and consulting with the state prescription monitoring website were implemented. These opioid safety initiatives were explained to the patients. Letters went out to every patient on opioids for chronic pain to explain the safety changes. Letters went out to the community and politicians explaining what the changes were and why, all in relation to saving lives. Unfortunately, reducing opioid levels often resulted in political and media scrutiny on the facility. Dissatisfied patients expressed their dissatisfaction through a number of channels including surveys, complaints to patient advocates, complaints to politicians, and direct contact with primary care and executive leaders. Some patients picketed. Other patients threatened violence and legal action. Mr. Director expressed his displeasure regularly.

Primary care providers and other clinical leaders perceived that the executive leadership team favored patient satisfaction over patient safety. I raised my concerns regularly to the executives, and I intervened regularly in the name of patient safety. Two of my primary care providers testified and supported their concerns.

Two days after returning from leave and immediately following the television news story, the chief of staff and medical director suspended my medical privileges stating I "failed to implement opioid safety initiatives in a safe and ethical manner."

The Professional Standards Board (PSB) unanimously recommended reinstatement of my privileges and forwarded the recommendation to the clinical executive board (CEB). The CEB approved reinstatement of my privileges. Eventually, Mr. Director and Dr. Chief of Staff conceded and the notice read, "Based upon the results of the comprehensive review there are no concerns that aspects of (my) clinical practice do not meet the accepted standards of practice. Therefore, I am happy to inform you that your clinical privileges have been fully restored effective immediately." This process took a nail-biting month. This outcome to this day has not been acknowledged by the Ignorant Oversight Body (IOB), the television news station which has the story accessible to the public to this day, the politicians involved, or the headquarters' president. The judge stated the information above; but he failed to realize the IOB report was faulty. The judge failed to realize "based upon the results of the *comprehensive review* there are *no concerns* that aspects of (my) clinical practice do not meet the accepted standards of practice." To conclude, the Ignorant Oversight Body failed to redact their allegations and instead, built a second investigation on their faulty original conclusions. This time, the IOB went after Dr. Chief of Staff. His perjured testimony and failure to address the IOB's faulty report landed him in the hot seat.

In the summer of 2017, Dr. Chief of Staff issued me a reprimand, stating failure to follow medical center policy which did not exist until 2018. I sent a lengthy reply, and my reprimand was reduced to a letter of counseling which was still unfair.

Realizing I would continuously be ducking retaliatory actions by the director and chief of staff, I understood I could not return to the facility. I tried to relocate to another facility, but my suspended privileges led to the East Coast Medical Center choosing their second-choice candidate. The other locations who were interested failed to hire me. I suspect the national attention I received made me an undesirable employee within the large health-care system. This became obvious. I was forced to retire. No one in their right mind would go back to the hostile environment I faced. My colleagues confided in me regularly, validating my concerns. The judge did not acknowledge this fact in the end, much to my frustration.

I previously filed a complaint with the Equal Rights Organization who accepted my case, stating my work environment met the requirements of being seriously hostile. This was overlooked during the presentation of my case; but we only had two days to outline a multitude of disclosures I made, to present the documentation, to provide testimony by witnesses, and to tie the overwhelming amount of documentation together.

The judge outlined applicable law, including the Whistleblower Protection Enhancement Act of 2012 (WPEA). He addressed my allegations regarding the agency and retaliation by leaders for my protected disclosures. The judge concluded that I showed by preponderant evidence I made protected disclosures.

I generally identified nine disclosures I made on various occasion over a two-year period to the chief of staff regarding opioid prescription issues, opioid overprescribing, improperly trained physicians, and improper influence on medical decisions or opioid safety plans. I made disclosures to the medical director also. I established by preponderant evidence to have made protected disclosures which I believed violated law and/or a substantial danger to public health or safety.

To my frustration, the judge did not acknowledge gross mismanagement or abuse of authority. In my opinion, the director, chief of staff, and politician clearly abused their positions of power in influencing primary care providers to change opioid prescriptions to make patients happy. I believe any clinician would clearly agree. I believe most people would agree; but obviously, not everyone sees clearly.

The judge reviewed all of my disclosures. As he reviewed the disclosures I reported to Dr. Chief of Staff, he included Dr. Chief of Staff's acknowledgment of the disclosures on each occasion. The judge referred to my testimony repeatedly. I clearly referred to Dr. Chief of Staff's actions as posing a risk to patient safety and violation of the law. Disclosures concerning interference in patient safety by the patient advocates, reports of drug dealing by patients to the to the police in the emergency department, reports about angry patients threatening staff to the police, disclosures made regarding Dr. Chief of Staff's unwanted involvement in reversing opioid tapers or reinstatement of opioids in unsafe situations were reviewed by the judge. The judge confirmed credible witness testimony of two primary care providers I supervised. He admitted both physicians testified that I was knowledgeable about opioid practices. They cited specific instances about visits or calls from Dr. Chief of Staff, strongly suggesting they change their treatment plans despite drug-seeking behaviors and other "red flags." One of the witnesses named Ms. Congresswoman and her role in practicing medicine without a license and undesirable influence by Dr. Chief of Staff. Dr. Chief of Staff ultimately agreed that he was responsible for the treatment of all of the hospital's patients, and he "got involved when he determined it was necessary to do so."

I referenced at the end of *Slaying the Dragon, Uncovering the Things They Like to Hide* that the Office of Inspector General (OIG) issued a report in June 2019, just before I submitted my second book for publishing. This timing of the release of the report and failure for the judge to release a timely report from the Legal Battle Board proceedings proved to be a gift from God. My attorney submitted the report to the Legal Battle Board for inclusion. Despite the agency's objections, the judge accepted the report. I believe the report contributed to the success of my case. I honestly did not believe the judge would be fair ultimately. I witnessed many unfair, untruthful, and perjured reports by the organization who, by the way, oversees the organization and protects itself ultimately from a damaged reputation. The organization puts laws, policies, procedures, oversight bodies (such as the Ignorant Oversight Body, Grievance Division Office, Complaint Department, Equal Rights Organization) and agency boards without members to ultimately decide rulings upon appeal. Whistleblowers spend time, money, more time, and more money for attorneys to expose unsafe, unlawful, dangerous, unethical, immoral, untruthful, and unprofessional practices by leaders wearing the institution's values on their chests but fail to model. I am thankful that the judge proved me wrong. In the end, the judge concluded I made "specific protected disclosures to (FBTRHCS) leadership relating to opioid prescription issues, including opioid over-prescription, diversion, improper provider training on urine drug screens, and improper influence on medical decisions or opioid safety plans." He concluded "based on the record evidence" that I "reasonably believed that (my) disclosures evidenced potential violations of law and a substantial and specific danger to public health and safety." He concluded I showed that I "engaged in protected activity." Glory to God in the highest.

The judge backed his decision referring to the law. To my relief, he stated my "whistleblowing was a contributing factor in some of the personnel actions at issue." He supplied legal justification. The judge listed three specific actions found to have established preponderant record evidence establishing the knowledge/timing test as to the personnel actions: First, Mr. Director issued me a notice of summary suspension of health-care privileges. Second, the agency removed me from my position as opioid safety initiative facility co-champion. Third, Dr. Chief of Staff issued me a notice of proposed reprimand for failure to follow medical center policy related to opioid prescription, mitigating the proposed reprimand to a letter of counseling about one month later. The three listed actions were considered "personnel actions" as defined by law. He clearly upheld points number one and number two. Point number three ended up falling out of his favor, at least to my understanding up to page 29 of 70 pages of the ruling.

The judge did not believe I had a firm job offer at the East Coast Medical Center by the evidence presented and based upon knowledge of protected disclosures or application of protected disclosures. He references the Media News story and PSB support, but these are not protected disclosures under the law. I accepted this just fine. The next statements upset me.

The Media News story and the agency's participation were not considered protected disclosure or activity attributed by me. And then there it was, the Ignorant Oversight Body report. The judge referenced the faulty report as fact. This faulty report which ignored clinical testimony, ignored the clinical reviews where I was found to be 100 percent complaint with tapers, ignored the fact that I had been covering providers in place to meet with patients face-to-face if the patients chose to, ignored the fact that the report was released two months prior to my suspension of privileges (which was in reality in response to the Media News story and my attorney solicited testimony by the director stating "staple the story to the suspension" and "we need to send a message (of fear)," and I wrote the action plan two months prior. How could the judge miss the retaliatory comments by my brilliant attorneys? The judge basically said, "Suck it up, Buttercup!" He did not believe I worked in a hostile environment despite the fact that the Equal Rights Organization stated my working environment clearly met the definition of a severe hostile environment. It amazes me that one person or one group can reach a conclusion that completely opposes another person's or group's conclusions. I know the environment was hostile. The environment crippled me. My clinical colleagues recognized the hostile environment. Multiple colleagues left the facility or changed positions to avoid the executive leadership team. Ultimately, the judge could not include suffering from a hostile work environment as not listed under a "personnel action" by law. Okay, I'll accept that statement; but don't tell me I should have sucked it up. Sucking it up would have resulted in a loss of my license in the end and loss of an important career. The threat was real.

The judge wrote that I "failed to establish by preponderant evidence that (my) retirement was involuntary." Again, we will need to agree to disagree. The "suck it up" mentality hits again. No physician voluntarily retires, three months shy of a full retirement with a

$1,700 monthly loss of income for the rest of her life. A physician involuntarily retires to protect her license from leaders with selfish ambitions willing to lie and bully their way to the top of some ladder (to nowhere in my opinion). A physician involuntarily retires to guard her medical license to maintain her ability to practice medicine and provide for her family, friends, and charitable organizations. A physician involuntarily retires to seek an environment free from (or at least reduced) retaliation for practicing safe, legal medicine and an environment free from hostility and public humiliation.

When Media News aired their story filled with untruths by patients, the aftermath was too much to negotiate. I became unemployable by other facilities in the organization. I believe my attorneys and I presented preponderant evidence of involuntary retirement. However, I believe the settlement would have been too onerous on the part of the organization. The judge need not have been concerned about the settlement. I knew all along that the agency would be able to appeal, and appeal they did on December 31, 2019, the last day set by the judge. There are now three vacancies on the appeals board. All of our country's Legal Battle Board rulings that have been appealed sit in a room, no doubt stacked to the ceiling covered by a thick coating of dust and cobwebs. The whistleblowers wait; but we don't hold our breath. The appeals board has been unable to rule on thousands of cases because the senate has not appointed board members for eight years now and counting.

CHAPTER 2

PROGRAMS FOR VETERANS AND BEYOND

I helped to initiate and implement a patient therapeutic riding and driving program for veterans with the executive director and assistant of Pegasus Farm. The idea started when Mark and I attended an event at Pegasus Farm in May of 2007. I sought out the executive director, Jim Strang, to introduce myself and express my interest in Pegasus Farm for veterans. He later shared through a letter that Pegasus was awarded a grant from the Austin Bailey Health and Wellness Foundation from Canton, Ohio, that would make the program available to veterans at no cost to them. Congressman Ralph Regula had been working with Jim Strang prior to my entrance to help finish the details that enabled the program to come to fruition. We were on our way to providing veterans the benefits of equine therapy. The program became fully functional, and it became an exciting method to help patients with a variety of physical and mental handicaps. I worked closely with the executive and program directors of Pegasus Farm and another coworker, Dianne Pryce, LISW, MSSA, to bring this program to our patients. We developed a referral history and physical form to be completed by a medical provider. We developed eligibility requirements for participants, informed consent forms, liability and release signature forms, and photo release forms. I immediately began referring my patients to the program. One of my patients would stop by to show me the ribbons he received through Pegasus Farm competitions year after year. I beamed with delight every time he stopped by.

As written in the Pegasus Farm program for disabled American veterans,

> Equine assisted activities are specifically designed for each individual participant to promote improvement in physical, psychosocial, and cognitive skills depending on the individual's need. Therapeutic riding provides an enjoyable and relaxing experience that provides the additional physical benefits through the natural input received astride the horse whose flowing, multi-dimensional movement replicates that of a human. The motion of the horse re-creates in the human the normal walking gate. Therapeutic driving provides the benefits of equestrian activity for those whom riding would not be recommended or simply for any individual interested in learning an equestrian skill other than riding.

The Horsemanship Course is an "unmounted equestrian activity" promoting "personal growth and a sense of accomplishment as the individual learns to handle and care for their equine partner."

I received a letter from James. W. Strang, executive director, dated June 15, 2007. "Dear Dr. Drumm, we are so excited that our Therapeutic Program for Veterans is finally up and running. Thank you for helping us turn this dream into a reality." To God be the glory!

When morale became low at Canton VA Community-Based Outpatient Clinic (CBOC), I scheduled our providers for "a day at the farm" retreat. It tickled me to watch the medical providers wander into the stables to check out the horses and become more comfortable with them as time passed. I remember it was a great day and that I brought cowboy hats for us all to wear that day.

Pegasus Farm

Veterans Salute!

A Therapeutic Equine-Assisted
Activities Program
for
American Veterans

Got Mail? Army veteran
Jim Myers and Kozy

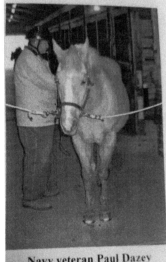

Navy veteran Paul Dazey
"tacking up" his horse

Army veteran Penny Dodrill
driving Wilbur with the supervision of NARHA certified Driving Instructor Diana Beardsley

From a Veterans Salute! Pegasus Farm brochure

I served as medical advisor for Honor Flight CAK. This group helped bring World War II veterans to see the memorials in Washington, DC. It was a fairly new program at that time, and I helped staff who traveled with veterans to the memorials and provided medical care or advice to those who became ill. Even though my schedule was often demanding, I continued to find time and energy to help with projects that helped to make the world a better place. I successfully recruited other VA staff nurses to volunteer for Honor Flight CAK. I observed one nurse develop her own goals, and she encouraged other nurses to participate. She told veterans about the program and excited them. We worked together on this project to serve our veterans in an exciting manner.

Earl Morse and Jeff Miller, cofounders Honor Flight Network

I helped to develop and lead educational challenges at the VA. The *Tele-dermatology Program* came into existence because of a research project that was created by a group of specialists at the organization. The group included me in their plans. I participated in a study that ultimately was published. I learned a new photography system, and I taught others how the equipment could be used to take photographs from a remote location and attach them to a medical chart. Primary care providers placed a "consult to the specialist" at a central location. The specialist reviewed the photographs and provided expert advice by written communication using the computer. Patient satisfaction was optimal. Most patients did not like to drive great distances to see a specialist. As gasoline prices increased, cost for travel became an added barrier. Because of our success, I was asked to train other providers in basic dermatology procedures and photography techniques. The tele-dermatology system functioned from most of our thirteen outpatient clinics. I had the exciting opportunity to be involved at the ground level of this innovative consultation process.

Pregnancy Support Center (PSC) embraced me as a volunteer. These faith-based staff and board members appreciated my passion to serve with enthusiasm. At the time I served at PSC, I continued my education as part of Baldwin Wallace College MBA in Healthcare program. I hoped to help bring PSC to a new level of community service as the medical arm of the center crossed new horizons.

Realistically speaking, I expected to stay at the VA for the rest of my medical career. As badly as I wanted to leave at times and as often as I placed one foot out the door, I really believed I would survive. I developed a real heart for veterans. The patients valued me overall. Not all patients liked me of course, but those who did expressed their appreciation openly. I received warm hugs and handshakes daily. Patients sent me cards and gave me tokens of appreciation such as vegetables from their gardens, cakes baked by their spouses, woodwork knickknacks they made from their shops, knitted coasters, stuffed animals, hats, war memorabilia, and more angels than I could display. I saved everything with a sense of pride, the good kind if it exists. I cherished each moment I spent participating in a parade or attending a community gathering with my patients. How many doctors get to develop this type of relationship with their patients?

Gifts received from patients and colleagues: frogs and Lori L. plaque by Doy Coyle; arc from Dr. Kabadi, Endocrinologist; heart by Paul Masalko, WWII veteran; Big Shot Doctor from James Mapes on 8-28-2007, angel from Lewis McClure May 2004, not pictured is a hummingbird given to me from Victor Dossi on 2/12/2008, and more.

Personally, at that point in my life, I lived on a twenty-acre farm with my wonderful husband, three horses, seven dogs, and two cats. Who could move? The tremendous amount of effort involved to relocate involved one serious pay increase (which tended not to be of great importance to me) or a leadership position where I would make more of a difference in the lives of others than I could where I lived at that time. As I developed additional business skills, advancement opportunities in teaching and employment arose. I entertained any offer that enabled growth and change for the betterment of society which sounds lofty now; but at that time, I really believed in doing my best to help make the world a better place to live, at least in my small area of influence. At that time, my volunteer participation continued to satisfy my service desires. I tried to increase my time spent on activities that enriched the lives of those around me. By serving others, God rewarded me. Leadership came naturally to me when I spent time at PSC. My efforts were appreciated and valued by faith-based organizations.

Photograph taken by Maxwell Leibsla, Lori and Mark, Katrina, Rusty, Cowboy, Knickers, Ginger, PA (Patience is not in the photo.)

I found an old leadership development plan I thought would share.

Ideals (stretch goals) ten to fifteen years out:

1. Politics (really? I chastise myself for this goal in retrospect)/ governmental (really?) program planning, probably health-care related, large health-care system related, innovative programs
2. Long-term facility care manager
3. Teaching
4. Caregiver (financial, possibly physical) for my mother
5. Develop land investment

Objectives three to five years out:

1. Serve on PSC financial planning board
2. Help expand PSC to other cities
3. Recreational vehicle uses at college campuses, other areas/ PSC
4. Teach at a college (start part-time)
5. Clarify vision about use of land investment

Goals one to three years out:

1. Finish MBA
2. Continue to teach at PSC
3. Continue to volunteer at PSC, Pegasus, Honor Flight, agency programs
4. Speak when asked—have a speaking engagement planned for October; speak at PSC
5. Attend board meetings, functions, outings
6. Attend State Round Table function
7. Work on community outreach programs
8. Pay down debt-fight for GI Bill extension, pay off vehicles, land, etc.

At that time, I thought about the means to accomplish my goals. I planned to expand my volunteer efforts at Pregnancy Support Center. Because this is a faith-based organization, I clearly felt led to serve there in a greater capacity. The staff welcomed my participation and appreciated me as a person in addition the skills and abilities I brought to the center. I enjoyed every moment I spent with my colleagues. I referred other friends with enthusiasm because I understood how enriching the experience could be working with others at this location. I volunteered performing ultrasounds on clients, served on the board, and acted as the medical director of PSC. Often limited by time due to other activities such as school and work, I hoped to possibly someday create a paid position at the center so that

I could spend more time there or decrease time requirements elsewhere to increase my volunteer time. As silly as it sounds, the pursuit of money was not at the top of my list. I desired to help in the pursuit of a greater good that did not have a worldly dollar value. Money was great and served a purpose. Without it, I could not have afforded to volunteer, so I did understand that a balance must exist. I stayed at the VA because working there allowed me to receive a good income at a job with good hours, allowing me to pursue other challenging endeavors; and above all, the veterans were worth serving!

Professional teaching, public speaking, community outreach volunteering, and academic achieving remained as immediate goals achievable within one to three years. Because of my job at the VA, I met patients who held offices with the Disabled American Veterans, American Legion Posts, Veteran Service Commission, and other veteran groups. The leaders often invited me to speak at holiday gatherings, dinners, events, parades, and programs. As a Navy veteran, I enjoy donning my uniform (that still fits by the way, well, maybe not now without a lot of Spanx) and participating. My patients smiled with pride because I was their doctor. Most of the veterans were elderly and thought I was young and pretty at that time of my life. I appreciated any compliment I received. I felt appreciated, respected, and valued.

Continuing classes in finance and finishing the MBA in health care enabled me to understand the business side of medicine. As I struggled with balance sheets and income statements, financial ratios, and *Capsim* simulations, I told myself that I needed to know this material. I enjoyed learning, even when the terms were foreign to me. Using the material and struggling to really learn enabled me to earn the credentials and apply the concepts to real working situations. PSC invited me to join their financial planning board when I felt more confident. The financial consultant appreciated my questions when I called her on several occasions regarding a school assignment pertaining to analysis of PSC's financial statements. I spent hours peering over old board notes to understand the numbers and flow of the spread sheets. I did not consider this a waste of time, knowing that I would someday be of assistance to the center. Once, a board member of PSC joked about me going back to school and asked me why I would undertake such a difficult endeavor when I was already a doctor. I think they now know why, and I laugh remembering this comment.

I had a dream about future expansion of Pregnancy Support Center. Following the purchase of a recreational vehicle (RV) to use to help Hurricane Katrina victims in 2005, I tried to think of other uses of the vehicle. I donated the use of the RV for fundraisers and set up the vehicle at a camp ground offering free horseback riding, four-wheeling, and other activities. Then I saw an RV set up in another town being used to provide pregnancy ultrasounds at satellite locations. This idea excited me. I spread the excitement to others at PSC. The only thing missing in the equation was time on my part to implement the program. Within three to five years, I hoped to carve out enough time to put the idea into action. Other board members started planning a site for Massillon. During the time spent on the recent assignment that I previously referenced, I discovered that many PSC clients come from Massillon. By placing the RV at a predictable site at regular intervals, others may be reached in their own community. College campuses needed services also. Many college parking lots could serve as satellite locations to reach this needy group of young women and would help outreach efforts to expand the services offered by PSC. In the end, PSC found a brick-and-mortar location to serve clients in Massillon.

To this day, I still own the RV. My husband and I towed it behind us as I wrote some of this book on our way home to Ohio to visit our family. It came in handy to travel to see my mother with a recently diagnosed B-cell lymphoma during the COVID-19 pandemic. We also used the RV during our moves with eight dogs (yes, we gained another dog) and two cats to Des Moines, Iowa, and Fort Wayne, Indiana, as I stepped into leadership administrative positions within the Department of Veterans Affairs at that time of my life.

I hoped to teach at the college level. Malone College would have been ideal. The executive director at PSC is married to a

Malone College administrator. I am well known to a congressman who may have been on staff at this college at that time. I know he was associated with the school. Again, through my job at the VA, I welcomed the opportunity to develop an indirect relationship with this important person, mostly through work opportunities but also through volunteer projects.

My staff at the clinic constantly reinforced my desire to teach. I enjoyed coaching and mentoring nurses and medical students. Many opportunities presented themselves for teaching in one way or another. Following the development of a *tele-dermatology* program at the large health-care organization, an administrator asked me to teach other primary care providers biopsy surgical techniques and photography skills. This request created some job satisfaction at a critical point in my career at the large health-care system.

My goal was to send out my resume to all of the osteopathic medical schools following completion of my MBA degree in addition to local colleges seeking my qualifications. I never became a college professor, but I did oversee VA Central Iowa Health Care System's medical student and internal medicine rotation programs while serving as the Primary and Specialty Care Service Line director for five years. Additionally, I spoke at the neighboring Des Moines University Osteopathic Medical School on occasion, which proved satisfying.

My husband and I purchased sixty acres of land eleven miles from our twenty-acre horse farm. We had a vision that was vague at that point in our lives of what we planned to do with the land. The country setting was perfect for some type of retirement, rehabilitation, special home, or other facility environment. The vision was not yet clear to us as to what we would do with the land.

Since owning the land, we purchased the original homestead and ten additional acres at an auction. Our sons and friends lived on the homestead on and off over time. Local farmers used our land for feeding their cows which helped them financially and enabled the property to be used agriculturally and proved to be a good investment over time.

An ideal goal during my MBA college days entailed a career in politics or governmental position related to health care. This completely makes my skin crawl at this point in my life; nonetheless, I acted on this desire at the time. Because I served my country as an active-duty officer, worked in private solo general medical practice, experienced the bureaucracy of the Department of Veterans Affairs, worked in the dental field for eight years, and sought business knowledge, I hoped to qualify to serve our country again in a different capacity. By understanding the health-care system, I hoped other leaders would recognize my enthusiasm, optimism, and motivating leadership style. Unfortunately, I realized that I sometimes did not fare well under the banner of a bureaucratic system; but I possessed the determination and self-confidence to win battles that had the potential to be perceived as valuable by others with similar moral and ethical standards. Ultimately, I believe God steered me far away from a political career, at least as an employee on Capitol Hill. Thank you, Jesus!

Mark and I experienced the tragic death of our son, Matthew, in August 2005. During our grieving process, we dove into the therapeutic calming effect of working with our horses and sought lessons from a local trainer. Additionally, we channeled our grief into helping Hurricane Katrina victims in Mississippi and Louisiana. *The Repository* featured this story and placed a gigantic photograph of me covering the full page. Donations poured in. The best donation ended up being influenza vaccines from the local hospital. We were able to provide medications in the form of samples by drug companies. I donated my office exam tables, otoscope, ophthalmoscope, exam stools, and other items from my private practice that were simply collecting dust in storage. We bought a toy hauler recreational vehicle (RV) to bring items down south. The RV also served as a place for us to stay. At the time, volunteers needed to be self-sufficient. Our two trips down south provided comfort to us. In serving others, we received blessings.

The Repository, Tuesday September 20, 2005

CHAPTER 3

COMMUNITY EVENTS

Patients began inviting me to community events. The community groups sponsoring events featured me, their doctor. My first speaking engagement was to take place in Malvern, Ohio. It thrilled me to receive recognition in the small-town newspapers.

Tom Burkhardt and Lori Drumm, Malvern,
Memorial Day, May 29, 2007

Memorial Day Speech by Lori Drumm, D.O. Monday May 28, 2007, Malvern, Ohio:

GOD BLESS AMERICA

And GOD BLESS all of you today on this Memorial Day holiday also known as Decoration Day. It is a day of remembrance to those who have died serving our nation. It is a general human need to honor our dead. Gathering together is a good way to honor our fallen heroes who gave their all, their lives, for our country and for the freedoms we all enjoy. Although traditional observance of Memorial Day has decreased over the years, I am proud to say that the city of Malvern has not forgotten the importance of this day. It is a thrill to be asked by The American Legion Valley Post #375 to be a part of Malvern's services. The breakfast, parade, prayers, speeches, salutes, band presentations and lunch plans speak volumes about the dedication of the veterans and other people in this area who worked so hard to prepare for this celebration. I feel truly privileged to be included in the events of this Memorial Day in Malvern.

The first celebration of this holiday took place May 30, 1868 at *Arlington National Cemetery* where both Confederate and Union soldiers were buried. Southern women decorated the graves of soldier even before the Civil War's end. Today, national observance of the holiday is still held at *Arlington National_Cemetery* with the placing of the wreath on the *Tomb of the Unknown Soldier* and the decoration of each grave with a small American flag. As we see the American Flag flying high, I hope we continue to remember those brave soldiers who fought so valiantly for our country and gave meaning to the "Land of the Free" and "Home of the Brave."

This holiday has meaning for me in so many ways. When I was just a young girl, I remember watching the news pertaining to Vietnam. At the time, silly as it sounds, I remember the *Sonny and Cher Show* and the segment discussing POW bracelets because my mother had the same POW as either Sonny or Cher. I had and still have my POW bracelet. Major Robert Rousch is a veteran I personally honor today. He was born in Hicksville, New York on May 22, 1938 and began his Vietnam tour April 16, 1970. His casualty date is October 9, 1973. He was thought to have died while missing from an air crash landing in Laos. His body was never recovered. The Vietnam War obviously left quite an impression on me. I truly believe that since childhood, I wanted help soldiers in some way

It is amazing how God works. I almost joined the armed forces on two previous occasions; but something else in life took precedence. I ended up in medical school shortly after The Persian Gulf War began on August 2, 1990. When the conflict culminated in fighting in January and February 1991, I took an oath to serve my country in the Navy. I just had to do something; it was time to make my country and the armed forces a priority in my life. Fortunately for our fighting service men and women at the time, a cease fire was declared on February 28, 1991. Thanks to a Health Professions Scholarship Program (HPSP), I finished medical school. Even though I was not a part of actual combat, I proudly served my country stateside as a general medical officer taking care of active duty, their families, and retired veterans at Groton Submarine base in Connecticut. Following four short years of private practice, I ended up serving military personnel once again at Canton VA Clinic where I currently provide medical care to our veterans.

I have had the privilege to meet many of our war veterans. I have personally heard many amazing stories of bravery by my patients. I have cared for WWII veterans who have stormed the beaches of Normandy, fought as tail-gunners on many dangerous missions, survived after their ships were sunk in Leyte Gulf and Pearl Harbor, and lived through indescribable conditions as Prisoners of War. Korean veterans, Vietnam veterans, Persian Gulf War veterans, and now Iraq and Afghanistan War veterans have also shared their experiences. What a blessing and an honor to learn of combat veterans' conquests and survival, family at home that supported them, and life upon return to the United States. I was thrilled to see a couple of veterans that I met yesterday in *The Canton Repository* Building. How thrilling it is to learn of their experiences and to see them receive the attention and respect that each soldier deserves. My husband and I have adopted another soldier who is presently stationed in Iraq. We met him when he was home on leave and now, we enjoy sending him care packages filled with ATV and four-wheeler magazines, candy, and other fun stuff that we hope he and his unit enjoy. There are so many soldiers today still defending our country in Afghanistan and Iraq as well as around the world. [HOLDS UP

LISTS OF NAMES] I hold up the names of those young men and women who have died just this past year defending our country to keep us safe from terrorists and other threats worldwide. About 1000 men and women died last year. We must continue to recognize and applaud their service to this "One Nation under God." Their families and friends must be so proud of them. Let's take a moment to express our gratitude to the families and friends who have lost a beloved serviceman or woman at any point in time with our hands. [PAUSE AND CLAP] Praise God for you and the strength, courage, and honor you represent through your loved one and in their memory today. I think those who are here today truly care about remembering our fallen veterans.

I cannot close this address without expounding on the important role each of you play in the support of a family member or loved one in the military. Those of you who are left behind are so vital to the morale of the service member. Letters, phone calls, emails, care packages, and prayers mean so much to the man or woman stationed away from home. Those of you who pay the bills, raise the children, go to work every day for a paycheck, and keep the household running in anticipation of a returning loved one are God's blessings. I hope you feel appreciated. And to you who have lost a loved one, whether to war or to other causes, I understand deeply. My husband, Mark, and I lost a 23-year-old son to a violent tragedy just two short years ago. We know the pain endured to carry on with life. Our middle son, Mitchell, now 23 years old, just returned from direct combat in Iraq. [HOLDS UP PHOTO OF

MITCH] We are so very proud of him. You see, he left for Iraq within months of the traumatic loss of his brother and good friend, Matthew. Mitch's dedication to his country and fellow comrades is admirable. We did not know what the Lord had in store for our lives; but we did know one basic thing: *In God We Trusted*. Without our faith and trust in an all-knowing God who is still in control of this country, we never would have been able to endure the daily stress present while Mitch served in Iraq. We praise God that Mitch is now home in the United States. We plan to continue to support our son and other military personnel from the home front.

I've talked longer than I anticipated. I want to close by making one more point. Let's keep God as our protector for our country. If we honor Him and ask Him for His help, He is faithful. I want to live in a country that has the protective hand of God covering its leaders, citizens, and military operations. God Bless Our Fallen Heroes. God Bless America. Thank you and God Bless all of you.

I rode as the guest of honor in a shiny red convertible in the small-town parade. I enjoyed every moment of the day. Soon, other groups provided invitations of participation.

I met a young active-duty soldier, Mitchell Meredith, and his lovely wife that day. Mark and I made a note to ourselves to send Mitchell care packages. We loved sending service men care packages, and we must have sent Mitchell some because I received a thank you card from him in June. Mitchell wrote, "Well, you really don't know much about me so I will tell you a little." He shared that he served in Army since 1999 and had been away from home for three out of five years. He desired spending time with his family, his "lovely wife and two little girls, Ava and Riley," ages five and two years at that time. He grew up in Canton and went to McKinley. Go Dogs! He has three brothers and one sister. His parents celebrated over thirty-five years of marriage. Mitchell enjoyed fishing and riding ATVs. We sent him ATV magazines to enjoy in his care packages. He thanked me for sending the boxes. Receiving his card brought warmth to my heart. I appreciated hearing from him, especially since he had others in his life waiting for his precious cards and letters.

Lori Drumm with Mitchell Meredith and his wife

Bill and Barb Balogh gave this photograph to me of Alex and Timothy and the USS *San Juan*'s departure. It is hanging in my office at Deer Lodge Medical Center in Montana.

Nancy and Dale Dinger sent me a copy of an article in News Leader Photo/Todd Reed. Dale wrote, "This photo is out of the *Minerva* newspaper. Thought you might like to have it. Nice article and pictures! Dale Dinger (your patient)."

My patient, Russ Wood, framed a collage of the Malvern,
Ohio, event for me which hangs in my office presently.

Veterans Day (November 11, 2007), Mark and I attended community events whenever possible. This event honored Michael Gump. We enjoyed seeing people from the Canton VA at events, both coworkers and patients.

Janet and Royal Weisel and Lori Drumm

Mike Gump, guest of honor

Lori Drumm and Frank Turner, a patient

Frank often sent me Christmas cards and in 2005 wrote me a letter,

> Dear Dr. Drumm (my favorite doctor), What a pleasant surprise I had when I opened The Repository Tuesday, September 20 and saw an article about a good doctor and a GOOD person. I want to wish you the best of luck in helping the devastated region of our southern states. What a great humanitarian effort! I continue to look forward to being your patient and receiving your very kind care. Sincerely, Frank H. Turner.

He is presently living in Ohio, and we reconnected recently.

Faircrest Memorial Middle School presents "War Letters" on November 12, 2007.

This was the sixteenth year that Valerie Street Kinney celebrated Veterans Day at Faircrest Memorial Middle School with the students, staff, and veterans. I attended this celebration for the first time. The theme centered on letters that were written during wartime. The posting of colors, singing "Star-Spangled Banner" started the program. The students took over from here beginning with two third-grade students singing *Yankee Doodle Dandy* and the eighth-grade band played *Armed Forces on Parade* conducted by two USMC veterans. The sixth grade choir sang "American Heroes." Other students acted in the presentation reading war letters from the Revolutionary War, Civil War, WWI, WWII, Korean War, Vietnam War, Desert Storm, and Operation Iraq Freedom. The students sang songs, and the audience joined in to sing "Proud to be an American."

I recognized quite a few of my patients at the event. I also learned more about Pegasus Farm and at an event. I joined the group for a photograph that was featured on a brochure about Pegasus Farm.

My second invitation for speaking came from the Veterans of Foreign Wars organization.

VFW Speech, October 18, 2008:

Good evening and Happy Anniversary to the members of the Veterans of Foreign Wars of the United States. Originally founded in 1899 as the American Veterans of Foreign Service, the VFW now serves 2.4 million members at 8,500 posts around the world. You are unique in that you have honorably served in an area of conflict as a deployed service member. You risked your life for your country far away from the comforts of home and even a good meal or shower for longer periods of time than I can even imagine. As your website states, you are "members of (an) elite group with a common bond of experience forged in sacrifice and danger (that) bands together in an organization that provides comradeship, a voice for aspirations and a tool for chosen undertakings." From what I understand, you all have been bonding for 25 years. I consider it a privilege to speak with you tonight.

I've been involved in different veteran activities since I came to the VA in May of 2002. I recently represented the Navy in the Hall of Fame Parade along with other true heroes. Six Prisoners of War were on the float along with others who represented their military branches with pride. As the military float went down the parade route, the spectators, proud Americans, stood up and clapped, saluted, and cheered. Like "the wave" at a football or baseball game, citizens of Canton respectfully acknowledged the presence of true American heroes. I was touched by the patriotism. The POW veterans waved to the crowd, smiled with pride, and I must say I saw a tear or two…well, maybe they were my own. I was so proud and honored to be standing in such company. Sure, I served and served proudly, I even joined during wartime… But here I stood, in the presence of veterans of Foreign Wars, just like yourselves. We don't all earn your position of honor.

I'm not sure if you all know the recent statistics about the veteran population. 23.8 million veterans are living today, 7.5% are women. There are 37 million dependents of living and deceased veterans. This is about 20% of the United States population. Most veterans living today served during wartime. The average age of a WWII veteran is 84 years, Korean veteran 76 years, Vietnam veteran 60 years old, Gulf War veteran 37 years…and of course, Iraq and Afghanistan veterans, just young whipper snappers like many of you were when you went off to defend our country.

I work for the Department of Veterans Affairs (VA). I am not here to represent the agency by any means; but I am here to support all of you as you celebrate your anniversary. And let me also say, that I proudly serve some of you as my patients and I strive to deliver the best health care I can provide. Although the VA did not have the best reputation, I have seen many changes during my 6 ½ years at the agency. I am studying for a master of business administration in health care. The more I study, the more I appreciate the agency. Our computer system is state of the art. We have real time access to medical records which means that test results like labs and x-rays are immediately recorded and can be accessed by doctors to provide efficient care to you, their patient. We can show you your x-ray or EKG, the electric recording of your heart, right on our computers before you leave. We can look up what the specialist had to say from Cleveland or even that doctor in Florida you saw over the winter. Access to health care has improved tremendously. New qualifying veterans can get an appointment at one of the outpatient clinics within one month. Specialty appointments are being outsourced which means that we send patients locally for many specialty tests and services to eliminate wait times. The VA strives "to restore the capability of (patients) with disabilities to the greatest extent possible, and improve the quality of their lives and that of their families." The VA tries to "ensure a smooth transition for (patients) from active military service to civilian life," to "honor and serve (patients) in life, and memorialize them in death for their sacrifices on behalf of the Nations." These may just be words to some employees; but they are true goals to me. I am committed to serving patients. In fact, I joined the Navy during the Gulf War because I wanted to take care of military people as a physician.

It is amazing how God works. I almost joined the armed forces on two previous occasions; but something else in life took precedence. I ended up in medical school shortly after The Persian Gulf War began on August 2, 1990. When the conflict culminated in fighting in January and February 1991, I took an oath to serve my country in the Navy. I just had to do something; it was time to make my country and the armed forces a priority in my life. Fortunately for our fighting service men and women at the time, a cease fire was declared on February 28, 1991. Thanks to a Health Professions Scholarship Program (HPSP), I finished medical school. Even though I was not a part of actual combat, I proudly served my country stateside as a general medical officer taking care of active duty, their families, and retired veterans at Groton Submarine base in Connecticut. Following four short years of private practice, I ended up serving military personnel once again at Outpatient Clinic where I currently provide medical care to our patients.

I have had the privilege to meet many of our war veterans. I have personally heard many amazing stories of bravery by my patients. I have cared for WWII veterans who have stormed the beaches of Normandy, fought as tail-gunners on many dangerous missions, survived after their ships were sunk in Leyte Gulf and Pearl Harbor, and lived through indescribable conditions as Prisoners of War. Korean veterans, Vietnam veterans, Persian Gulf War veterans, and now Iraq and Afghanistan War veterans have also shared their experiences. What a blessing and an honor to learn of combat veterans' conquests and survival, family at home that supported them, and life upon return to the United States each soldier deserves.

My husband and I adopt soldiers who are stationed in Iraq. One we met when he was home and another is a patient of mine. We enjoy sending care packages filled with baby wipes, hand gel, tooth brushes, magazines, candy, and other fun stuff that we hope they will enjoy. There are so many soldiers today still defending our country in Afghanistan and Iraq as well as around the world. We must continue to recognize and applaud their service to this "One Nation under God." Their families and friends must be so proud of them. Praise God for you and the strength, courage, and honor you represent.

For those of you who may not have met my wonderful husband, Mark, let me introduce you now. He's a great man. Many people often ask him if he served. He smiles and says, no...but my wife and son have! Our middle son, Mitchell, now 24 years old, is now safely home after serving in direct combat in Iraq. [HOLDS UP PHOTO OF MITCH]

We are so very proud of him. You see, he left for Iraq within months of the traumatic loss of his brother and good friend, Matthew, who died from an unexpected tragedy. Mitch's dedication to his country and fellow comrades is admirable. We did not know what the Lord had in store for our lives; but we did know one basic thing: In God We Trusted. Without our faith and trust in an all-knowing God who is still in control of this country, we never would have been able to endure the daily stress present while Mitch served in Iraq. We praise God that Mitch is now home in the United States. We plan to continue to support our son and other military personnel from the home front.

I've talked longer than I anticipated. I want to close by making one more point. Let's keep God as our protector for our country. If we honor Him and ask Him for His help, He is faithful. I want to live in a country that has the protective hand of God covering its leaders, citizens, and military operations. God Bless Our Veteran Heroes from the present and the past. Each one of you here tonight put your life on the line to keep America safe. Without the dedication and service that each one of you gave, we would not be able to freely say, God Bless America. Thank you and God Bless all of you.

Mark and I enjoyed the banquet with all of the guests that evening. The following year, I received another invitation to speak. Preparation for the speeches became easier, especially for similar events.

Cathy, Dr. Al Wohlwend, Quartermaster Navarre
VFW Post 5047, Mark Leibsla

Cheryl Haswell, Junior Miller, John Rohrig, Lori Drumm

Chester Larson and his wife with Lori Drumm

Faircrest Memorial Middle School presents "The Spirit of America" on November 11, 2008.

This yearly event began with breakfast and then the posting of the colors by VFW Navarre Post 5047, John Rohrig, Ralph Rohrig, John Sukosd, John Jogerst, Albert Wohlwend, and Zach Griffith from the Civil Air Patrol. Many of these men were my patients and/or participated in community events with me. I recall these events with fondness and a smile.

Mr. Charles Dazey, USN Vietnam veteran, sang our national anthem and led us in the Pledge of Allegiance. Alexis Karovic and Breanne Lutz sang "You're a Grand Old Flag." The eighth-grade choir lead by Amy Bush sang "America, the Free." The sixth-grade choir sang "The Heart of America." The seventh grade choir sang the "Spirit of America," and we all sang, "Proud to Be an American."

There were performances, words of welcome and closing, and presentations by Brandy Yoho, Canton South High School graduate, class of 2008; Canton Elite Silver Stars directed by Karla Neff (performers were Ashley Eckroate, Lucy Thompson, Kaci Pledgure, Alex Garofal, Megan Maurer, and Brittany Miering); Mr. Tim Welker, Zach Griffith, and Mrs. Gay Welker. VFW Navarre Post 5047 retrieved the colors.

I enjoyed the event once again with veterans Frank Turner and Ralph Wellendorf, whom I served as their doctor. I also participated in other community events with others, including Al Wohlwend, John Jogerst, John Rohrig, Ralph Rohrig, at the VFW Post 5047 Veterans Day celebration and sixty-third anniversary dinner dance on October 18, 2008. Don Milliken attended the event. Ted Adamski, a highly decorated veteran, participated that day. I saw him regularly in parades, and we rode together in a parade in Harold Waldrop's WWII vehicle. I did not know anything about Don Milliken at that time other than he was a physical therapist. I learned more about him later. He served our country valiantly. We participated together serving veterans on Akron Canton Honor Flights. Bob Hahn was present that day unknowingly to me at that time. We rode together on the Canton Hall of Fame VA float together in uniform on August 2, 2008. Robert "Bob" R. Hahn served in World War II as a merchant mariner in the European Theater of the war.

Able SN Robert R. Hahn, Merchant Marine, Football Hall of Fame Parade 2008. Photo given to me by Robert Hahn.

Memorial Day speech by Lori Drumm, DO, Monday May 25, 2009, New Philadelphia, Ohio.

GOD BLESS AMERICA

And GOD BLESS all of you today on this Memorial Day holiday also known as Decoration Day. It is a day of remembrance to those who have died serving our nation. It is a general human need to honor our dead. Gathering together is a good way to honor our fallen heroes who gave their all, their lives, for our country and for the freedoms we all enjoy. Although traditional observance of Memorial Day has decreased over the years, I am proud to say that the city of New Philadelphia has not forgotten the importance of this day. It is a thrill to be asked by New Philadelphia VFW Post #1445 to be a part of today's services. The parade, prayers, speeches, salutes, and luncheon plans speak volumes about the dedication of the veterans and other people in this area who worked so hard to prepare for this celebration. I feel truly privileged to be included in the events of this Memorial Day in New Philadelphia.

I gave the history of the day's meaning using the same information I shared previously. I shared the history of my POW bracelet with Major Robert Rousch's name engraved on the treasured keepsake and how the Vietnam War affected me as a young girl. I spoke about serving as a general medical officer (GMO) at Groton Submarine Base in Connecticut and my transition to private practice and ultimately serving as a family doctor for veterans at the Canton VA.

A new community activity involved flying with Honor Flight CAK (HF CAK) with

World War II veterans to see their memorial in Washington, DC. I started off as a guardian for a veteran on oxygen, later served as a bus captain, and ultimately affectionately became the HF CAK medical officer.

My speech continued: My husband, Mark, and two stepsons, Mitchell and Maxwell, volunteer as a part of Honor Flight that currently brings WWII veterans and other terminally ill war veterans, free of charge, to see their memorials in Washington DC. I am certain we will learn of more heroic efforts this coming Saturday, May 30th and again on September 12th as we board the plane for our next trips to Washington from Akron Canton Airport. If you have never experienced a war homecoming, I invite each and every one of you to Akron Canton Airport at 8 pm to welcome the honored veterans returning from their day of honor. Many tears of joy are shed as the returning veterans receive the homecoming welcome for which they have waited for over 63 years.

Korean veterans, Vietnam veterans, Persian Gulf War veterans, and now Iraq and Afghanistan War veterans have also shared their experiences with me over the past 7 years I have worked at the VA. There are about 23.8 million living veterans today, 7.5% are women. There are about 37 million dependents, spouses and dependent children of living veterans and survivors of deceased veterans. Together, this represents 20% of the United State population. Most veterans living today served during times of war, the largest group are from the Vietnam War, about 7.9 million.

What a blessing and an honor to learn of combat veterans' conquests and survival, family at home that supported them, and life upon return to the United States. There are so many soldiers today still defending our country in Afghanistan and Iraq as well as around the world. [HOLDS UP LISTS OF NAMES] I hold up the names of those young men and women who have died just this past year defending our country to keep us safe from terrorists and other threats worldwide. About 4,300 men and women died since the war in Iraq began 3/19/03. Over 30,000 have been wounded. We must continue to recognize and applaud their service to this "One Nation under God." Their families and friends must be so proud of them. Let's take a moment to express our gratitude to the families and friends who have lost a beloved serviceman or woman at any point in time with our hands [PAUSE AND CLAP] Praise God for you and the strength, courage, and honor you represent through your loved one and in their memory today. I think those who are here today truly care about remembering our fallen veterans.

I shared our personal experience of dealing with the unexpected death of Matt and Mitch's bravery of serving in Iraq just a few months after the death of his brother and best friend. I thanked those who kept the home front going while the service man or woman served our country. Lastly, as always, I pled to keep God as the head of our country.

My speech ended, and Mark and I spent time speaking with many people attending the celebration and remembrance of those who gave the ultimate sacrifice for our country, their lives.

Faircrest Memorial Middle School presents "Do I Make You Proud?" on November 11, 2009.

I participated in posting of colors and retrieving of colors during this program along with John Rohrig, John Sukosd, Tom Wohlwend, and Zach Griffith. Kinney's kids, Mykle Lopp, Noah Mittas, Victor Rivas, Nathan Breinig, Sam Morgan, Ed Poland, Lyndsay Blackburn, Mrs. Davis, Miss Palmer led the Pledge of Allegiance. Chuck Dazey sang the national anthem. Alexis Karovic, a fifth grader, and Breanne Lutz, an eighth grader sang "God Bless Our Soldiers Tonight." Miss Bush directed the choirs. The sixth-grade choir sang "I Want to Thank You" and featured Jordan Smith, a seventh grader. The eighth-grade choir sang "Song of the Unsung Hero," and the seventh-grade choir sang "Do I Make You Proud." Mrs. Gay Welker provided closing remarks.

Valerie Street Kinney, Veterans Day chairperson and teacher of multiple disabilities, and others at Faircrest Memorial Middle School educated the students about the importance of remembering veterans and honoring their service to our country. Once I learned about the Veterans Day yearly programs, I attended. Many individuals and veteran organizations supported these yearly programs. The event involved vision, planning, organization, and reaching out to the veterans. Many people and organizations contributed finances, time, talent, and effort to prepare for the event and clean up afterward. I want to thank all of those people who contributed to the special yearly Veterans Day breakfast at Faircrest Memorial Middle School. Veterans appreciated all of your efforts. The yearly events provided a way for us to bond with the students, teachers, servers, presenters, and other veterans. We appreciated your service year after year. These programs impacted our hearts.

The history of Faircrest Memorial Middle School was dedicated in 1970 and the first principal, Mr. Ed Palmer, a Korean Army veteran, reminded the students of the nine soldiers for whom the school was named and included: Bill Joe Greavu, Army sergeant; Sharon Ann Lane, Army nurse, first lieutenant; William R. Masters, Army sp. 4; Fred Penland, Army PFC; Frank Sills, Marine PFC; Larry Rogers,

Army Spec. 4; David Brooks, Army PFC; Leonard Schoeppner, Navy lieutenant (MIA); and Benjamin Stoffer II, Army PFC. This impressed Valerie Street Kinney. During Mr. Palmer's tenure and following his retirement, he attended the yearly Veterans Day events.

During the 1990 to 1991 Desert Shield/Desert Storm, which is when I joined the Navy, Valerie and Mrs. Barbara Weaver encouraged students to make, package, and sell patriotic badges. They raised $1,200 in a few months. The war ended. Valerie and others started their first Veterans Day program in 1991. The program originally was planned for one year, but because of the gratitude expressed by the veterans, the program became a tradition to honor those who served. The school held a breakfast yearly, and every four years, they planned a school wide program. In a brochure I still treasure, Valerie thanks Mrs. Barbara Weaver (1939–2002), her first classroom aide and first assistant chairperson for the Veterans Day program in 1991. Barbara's husband served in Korea and supported the program. She thanked Mr. Jack Fuller (1955–2001), a former seventh-grade social studies teacher who helped create *More to the Wall than Just a Name* and volunteered until 2001. She thanked Mr. Tim Welker as their commander, Annette Davis, her good friend, and their master sergeant, who served since 1995, Mrs. Kathy Miller, their master chef, Ms. Debbie Elsas, their director and writer, and Ms. Amy Szwast, their art director and new recruit.

Ralph Rohrig, Lori Drumm, John Rohrig at Faircrest
Middle School Veterans Day school program

John Rohrig is still enjoying life in Ohio, and he is ninety years old on the day I am writing about him. I interviewed him by telephone recently. His brother, Ralph, passed away. He was four years older than John and served in Peacetime in Okinawa and worked with John at TimkenSteel.

SFC John Rohrig, born on September 16, 1920, served his country during the Korean War from 1952 to 1953. He was wounded in Korea, received a Purple Heart, and honorably discharged from the Army in 1953.

John and his wife married in 1962 and celebrated fifty-nine anniversaries. They have four sons. John worked as an overhead crane operator at the steel mill earning a retirement from TimkenSteel Corporation Company.

Faircrest Middle School Veterans Day school program

CHAPTER 4

HONOR FLIGHT NETWORK

Earl Morse, a retired USAF Captain and physician assistant, created Honor Flight Network in 2005 with the help of Jeff Miller, cofounder. Their mission was to transport America's veterans to visit their memorials in Washington, DC. Veterans received an all-expense-paid trip and an opportunity to share memories, experiences, and stories with other veterans. They often remembered comrades lost. As of May 14, 2011, the network had grown from 126 WWII veterans flown to Washington, DC, to over 63,000 veterans. The hubs grew from one hub in Ohio to 95 active Honor Flight hubs in 34 states. In 2019, 23,045 veterans flew to see their memorial and included 1,987 WWII veterans, 6,176 Korean veterans, 13,070 Vietnam veterans, and 1,812 other veterans. From 2005 to 2019, 245,178 veterans enjoyed one of the best days of their lives in the company of others who courageously served our great country.

Many generous donors contributed to the trip. Guardians paid their way for the trip and volunteered their time caring for the veterans they escorted. Whenever possible, the network encouraged family members who were physically able to accompany their family service member to become a guardian. Many family members never heard the veterans' experiences from wartime until the trip.

Medically trained guardians were also encouraged to volunteer. This is where my Honor Flight service began.

Companies, individuals, and military organizations gave generously to support the trips. I want to thank all the donors that gave to Canton-Akron (CAK) Honor Flight. Canton Community Based Outpatient VA Clinic donated the use of wheelchairs for many trips. I worked to get the chairs secured for the trips since I worked at this clinic as a physician. Honor Flight CAK, a 501(c)(3) nonprofit organization, consisted of big-hearted volunteers motivated by their love to serve veterans. Many families donated money in memory of their loved ones who passed away after having the incredibly amazing opportunity to be part of Honor Flight CAK. The Akron-Canton (CAK) Airport staff, Timken Company, J.M. Smucker Company of Orrville, US Airways, American Airlines, Marriott Hotels & Resorts, Aultman Foundation, Marathon Petroleum Company, Time Warner Cable, HBO, Miller Rentals, Canton South Men's Club, Business Cards Tomorrow of Ohio, Lake Professional Building, other groups and companies, and many individuals donated generously for the trips. Eighty-second Airborne Division Association, Disabled American Veterans, American Legion Posts, American Legion Riders squad, VFW Ladies Auxiliary Alliance, AMVETS, Veterans of Foreign Wars, North Central Ohio Ex-POW, Inc., Korean War vets, Rolling Thunder Ohio, and other groups donated generously also and gave the biggest welcome home celebration to the veterans upon their return to Akron-Canton Airport. Happy tears flowed from many of the veterans.

May 3, 2008, Honor Flight CAK

My first Honor Flight CAK trip took place on 5-3-2008 as a guardian with my husband, Mark. We attended guardian training prior to the trip where we learned about the history of Honor Flight, safety procedures, preflight duties, itinerary for the trip, and postflight duties. Bus captain duties required taking roll call, understanding

Honor Flight protocol, understanding bus tour plans, how to handle emergencies during the day if any, and how to direct any questions or concerns by travelers. Mark, a team captain, made sure the team was on the bus on time, reports the response from roll by announcing, "All present and accounted for," wheelchair accountability, communication with bus captains, and communication with team members. As a guardian, I was to be aware of my veteran's needs, make sure he had plenty of water, share facts about the memorial with my veteran, and take pictures of the veteran.

Our day began bright and early at 5:00 a.m. The veterans arrived at 6:00 a.m. I had the honor to meet PFC Arthur "Ack Ack" Cozza. Mark had the honor of meeting Glenn Carlisle, Robert Houghton, and Homer Marsh. We all spent time visiting; and I, of course, took a notable amount of video footage and snapped numerous photographs. We all boarded the plane at CAK Airport at 7:00 a.m. and departed by 8:00 a.m. Breakfast, provided by US Airways, was served on the airplane. As guardians, we all took advantage of the opportunity to visit with our veterans.

Arthur spent most of our time telling me about his Marine comrades being featured in an upcoming miniseries based upon his platoon and based upon the book, *With the Old Breed*, by E. B. Sledge. He told everyone he could about the miniseries directed by Tom Hanks and Steven Spielberg. His excitement captured the ear of many others during the trip.

Arrival at Regan National Airport started with a water cannon salute by fire trucks to honor the veterans, a ceremony unique to honoring military service, dignitaries, and people or groups of importance arriving in Washington, DC. Plumes of water engulfed the airplane, forming an arch of propelled water from the fire trucks. I cannot think of a more deserving group than these war veterans. As we departed the plane with our veterans, men and women in uniform greeted us as we made our way down the tarmac. The greeters shook the hands of each veteran as they passed by. Once inside the airport in Washington, DC, the massive crowd gave way to the veterans which reminded me of God parting the Red Sea for Israel's slaves fleeing from the Egyptians. The crowd shouted, "Thank you for serving!" and, "Welcome to Washington, DC!" as each individual attempted to shake the veterans' hands. The endless line of thankful citizens and people in uniform overwhelmed the veterans with their gratitude. This welcome surprised the humble group of veterans beyond words. I filmed the welcome, and to this day, I cannot believe God allowed me to serve such an amazing generation of veterans. I felt truly blessed.

Following bathroom breaks and boarding of the buses at Regan National Airport, we headed to the World War II Memorial. Senator Bob Dole greeted the veterans and gladly participated in photograph sessions with the veterans. His faithful presence in welcoming veterans to the WWII Memorial became notable at every Honor Flight trip I attended until he became ill. Elizabeth Dole took over greeting us. As part of Honor Flight CAK tradition, a flag ceremony took place at the Ohio pillar of the WWII memorial honoring a fallen veteran who would never be able to attend. The veterans ate lunch at the memorial, and then we boarded the bus to the Iwo Jima Memorial. A group photo took place at this memorial, and we took time to photograph our veterans. Next on the agenda involved boarding the bus again to visit the Vietnam Memorial, Korean Memorial, and Lincoln Memorial. I took advantage of photography moments which included spontaneous visits between Arthur and fellow Marines. The Marines seemed to instantaneously bond when they encountered each other, sharing their location during WWII.

Arthur continued to share that his unit was to be featured on the HBO miniseries, *The Pacific*. I did not realize how many times he shared this information until I watched all my videos from the trip in preparation for this book. Arthur Cozza was immensely proud of his unit.

Lastly, the veterans received a bus tour of Washington, DC, ending at Regan National Airport. Just when the group thought their day was ending, a nostalgic WWII dance company burst into song and dance playing music loved by this generation. The able-bodied veterans joined in the fun. Others received a kiss from a pretty girl and showed off the lipstick mark on their faces.

The welcome back to CAK Airport proved to be the most fantastic welcome-home celebration I ever witnessed. So many tears were shed by the veterans that night and by us as guardians. People filled the airport. Music played in the background. The crowd again parted like the Red Sea as the veterans deplaned and entered the terminal. You would never know it was about 10:00 p.m. at the end of an exceptionally long day for these eighty to ninety-plus-year-old veterans. I am certain they slept well that night. I know I did. My smile could not have been bigger as I thanked the Lord for the traveling mercies for all involved in the celebratory day.

Mark and I kept in contact with the veterans we met that first trip. I made photo albums for the veterans we cared for, and I received wonderful cards in return which I still cherish. Glenn Carlisle kept in touch for years and visited us in East Sparta one day. He raised $50,000 dollars for an outreach to Haiti in 2012. This money helped to dig a well for fresh water and assist schools. He raised money for all sorts of charities. He had cancer; but this didn't stop him from serving the Lord.

My relationship with Arthur Cozza and his family began on this trip and continued with his family after Arthur passed away in April of 2021. His passing spurred me to write this book about the heroes I served and the blessings I received.

Arthur Cozza, Lori Drumm, Glenn Carlisle,
Robert Houghton Homer Marsh

Veteran who survived Pearl Harbor, taken from my video camera

PFC Arthur Cozza, WWII Marine, at the WWII Memorial

Mark Leibsla, PFC Arthur Cozza, WWII veteran, Senator Bob Dole

The HF CAK veterans at the Iwo Jima Memorial, Yellow Bus

Glenn Carlisle from Goshen, Ohio

Two Marines connect at the Korean Memorial.

Robert Houghton, Lori Drumm, Arthur Cozza; Robert
ended up borrowing an electric wheelchair this day, and
we went crazy trying to find him. He had fun!

Gerald Meyer with family and friends
Gerald Meyer, USMC, Battle of Leyte, Philippines, WWII

September 22, 2008, Honor Flight CAK

I did not fly with this group of veterans; but I greeted them at CAK Airport when they arrived. I caught their entrance by video, and I included a couple of frozen shots from the video. I saw my patient, Mr. Paul Rodocker, arrive; and I introduced him to my husband, Mark. I greeted other guardians, such as Jim Jackson, Valere Turner, Tom Hutchinson, and Lori Hinderer upon their arrivals, along with the veterans. Many veterans shed tears of joy. One veteran could not speak because of his overwhelming emotions induced by the fanfare. Another veteran donned a Pearl Harbor survivor cap.

Flight 9090 from Akron Canton was honored to have T5 Marvin Hutto carry the flag from the family of Tech. 3C Ralph Stanich and place it in front of the Ohio pillar. Ralph served in Northern France. Ron Stanich, his son, is a retired USAF colonel. A wreath was then placed at the Field of Stars in remembrance of those who did not make it home.

Their day started at the World War II Memorial which honors the sixteen million who served and over four hundred thousand who died along with others that supported the war effort. They then went to the Iwo Jima Memorial, the United States Marine Corps War Memorial that remembers the historic battle on Mt. Suribachi. Next, the veterans and their guardians visited the Franklin Delano Roosevelt Memorial composed of four red granite galleries. President Roosevelt, Eleanor Roosevelt, and their beloved Scottish terrier, Fala, are some of the sculptures in the memorial.

A popular Honor Flight stop encompassed multiple memorials all within walking distance and/or wheelchair ride. The Korean Memorial depicts fighting men from the Army, Navy, Air Force, and Marines as they fought for victory. The wall of the memorial has over 2,000 photographs honoring supportive services. The Pool of Remembrance allows visitors to reflect on the loss of 54,246 American lives. The Vietnam Memorial includes the Three Soldiers statue, Vietnam Women's Memorial, and The Wall. More than 58,000 Americans died, and some are still unaccounted for. The Vietnam War affected me as a child, and I still have my POW bracelet honoring Major Robert Rausch. I wore it to many speaking engagements. I was proud to be co-captain with Pat Walker on some Honor Flights, a Vietnam corpsman and friend I admire. The Lincoln Memorial honors Abraham Lincoln, America's sixteenth president.

SGT1C Paul Rodocker, WWII, Army, my patient

Pearl Harbor survivor

Honor Flight CAK homecoming welcome overwhelmed a veteran

May 30, 2009, Honor Flight CAK

I had the honor to serve on Honor Flight CAK with Patrick Walker, Vietnam corpsman as co-bus captains for the red white and blue bus. My husband, Mark Leibsla, my stepsons, Mitchell and Maxwell, also served veterans on this trip. Mitchell is an Iraq veteran, and Maxwell is our official bagpiper for Honor Flight CAK.

Mark served as a guardian to Dean Meier and Donald Klein. Dean Meier served in WWII, along with his three brothers. Dean was born October, 28, 1922, and was part of WWII Air Corps Army. He also served in the Air Force Reserves. Donald "Don" Klein was from Canton, born November 29, 1925, and served in the Army. He received a Purple Heart and was missing in action while hospitalized in Paris. He served in Germany after the war.

Max served William Trolio, my patient from New Philadelphia Community-Based Outpatient Clinic, and Charles Kucyk. Both veterans served in the US Navy. Charles Kucyk, Navy seaman first class gunner enjoyed polka dancing. His family met him at the WWII memorial. His unit joined with a convoy and hauled cargo in Europe and the North Atlantic.

Richard Walker, born March 7, 1927, sat next to me at one point on this trip. He served in the Navy during WWII from 1944 to 1946 as a seaman first class boatswain's mate. His tour took him to the Pacific, Manila Bay, where he watched for submarines. As a seaman first class boatswain's mate, aboard a tanker filled with a billion gallons of gas, he and his crew supported fourteen planes on the deck. The crew took turns with watches as they manned and served as gunners. At one point, they rescued ten comrades who had to jump from a plane into the water below. Richard told me about his friend, Frank Miller, Air Force, from North Canton. The Japanese shot down Frank's plane, and he was rescued by the Japanese and taken to a concentration camp. When he was released, Frank weighed eighty-seven pounds. Richard teared up describing how it felt when the Japanese surrendered. Looking out the window of the plane over the clouds and the water as I listened, he said, "This flight is worth it." He then served during the Korean War from 1950 to 1952. He and his wife owned Minerva Airfield in Ohio.

I receive a thank-you note from Charles Kucyk written June 14,2009. He wrote,

> Dear Lori, I just want to send you my deep hearted thank you for the wonderful effort you gave toward making my Honor Flight trip to DC such a memorable experience. Enjoyable yes, but very emotional, the greetings we got at both airports on arrival were overwhelming, my tear ducts have been well flushed! And please thank your son, Maxwell, my guardian for his wonderful care and attention (when he could find me). I am happy to have met Mitchell and Mark, he sat next to me on the bus, and had his hands full, but did a great job. Your family is great, and I know you're proud of them. I am. Thanks again. Keep up the good work. Love ya all, Charles W. Kucyk.

My eyes were well flushed too!

My patient from Canton Community Outpatient Clinic, Joseph Nolan, flew on this day also. He sent me a card that said, "Dr. Drumm, I just want to thank you for the Honor Flight pictures. I was surprised to see you in Washington-you were the only one I knew on the trip. Again, thank you-see you in November. Joe Nolan." I loved running into my patients on the flights. Another one of my patients, Mr. Morehead, accompanied by Pam Overcasher, surprised me that day too.

Mr. Richard Robinson, another patient from Canton VA, sported a WWII cowboy hat. I enjoyed running into him during the trip. He sent me newspaper articles of different trips in the future when he discovered my name and photograph with a veteran.

This Honor Flight CAK started out early also. Veterans registered at 5:45 a.m., met their guardians, socialized, and took photographs. By 8:00 a.m., we all ate breakfast on the airplane as we headed to Reagan National Airport. The veterans received the water cannon salute by the fire department and deplaned, receiving a welcome they never expected. The entrance into the airport did not disappoint me. The men and women dressed in uniform positioned along the tarmac, extending their hands to shake the heroes' hands, the help from the pilot, flight attendants, and airport staff, the service organizations that lined the hallways of the airport, other travelers who went out of their way to welcome the veterans, bands that played patriotic music; and the dancers in attire from the 1940s never got old. It proved to be another day I had the privilege to take pictures of the veterans, record video footage, and serve the veterans with another veteran, Pat Walker, and my family.

Maxwell Leibsla, the bagpiper, led the veterans to the Ohio pillar of the WWII Memorial to place the flag of a fallen veteran. Wally Davis, a loyal guardian, placed his father's flag in front of the Ohio pillar that day. His father served in WWII. USN Fireman 1C Davis Jr. was stationed in the Pacific as a minesweeper. He and his crew landed in Japan soon after the atomic bomb was dropped.

I met Earl Roth, US Army medic, who was present during the Battle of the Bulge. He shared that he had tea with President Truman. Harry Schwab, USN, showed me a picture of a friend who died before having the opportunity to go on an Honor Flight. Harry brought him along in his heart that day.

Following the WWII Memorial, the group loaded the buses and headed to the Iwo Jima Memorial for a group photograph. The next stop was the Franklin Delano Roosevelt Memorial which occupies 7.5 acres. Famous quotes by the president are on the walls of the memorial which consists of four outdoor rooms representing the four terms served by the president. Sculptures line the memorial that illustrate the Depression and other themes. This memorial brought plenty of shade and a beautiful walk to be enjoyed by the veterans and their guardians.

The next stop included time at the Vietnam, Korean, and Lincoln memorials. We boarded the buses once again, sang "God Bless the USA" on the way back to Reagan National Airport, danced with the dancers at the airport, and flew back to Akron Canton Airport. Just as the veterans thought their day was done, Max, the bagpiper, led the group to the grandest welcome home of the veterans' lives. The expansive crowd cheered. The band played in the background. Spectators waved American flags; and red, white, and blue balloons filled the grand entrance to the airport. This group of veterans received a grand welcome home that was decades overdue.

Lori Drumm and William Trolio, USN, my patient from
New Philadelphia Community-Based Outpatient Clinic

Harry Schwab, USN. He brought a photograph of a friend,
who died, with him on the flight and showed it to me.

Richard Robinson, USAAC, with his son to his right,
Douglas Robinson, being greeted at the airport

I had the honor of serving Richard at the Canton VA. On August 22, 2009, Richard wrote me a letter and penned, "Wasn't it a great 'Honor Flight CAK' May 30, 2009? I was able then to pick up my brother's remains and then hold a memorial service with military honors at the family cemetery plot, August 6, 2009."

On October 2, 2009, I received a card with the following note,

> Dear Dr. Drumm, Honor Flight CAK May 30th 2009 was GREAT. A wonderful experience. Glad we could make it. It worked out very well. Especially glad Dick Walker made it before his death. Your pictures are greatly appreciated, you did a wonderful job. See you on the 20th of October. Thanks!! Sincerely, Dick Robinson.

Wally Davis III carried a photograph of his fallen veteran father, USN Fireman 1C Wallace Davis Jr. and placed a flag in front of the state of Ohio pillar, a tradition of Honor Flight to represent all those who never had the opportunity to see their memorial. Bagpiper Maxwell Leibsla to the right and CPL Walter Bauer and CPO QM Donald Miller to the left.

Richard Walker, WWII veteran with Mitchell Leibsla, Iraq veteran

Donald Morehead, USN, my patient at the clinic, with Pam Overcasher

Lori Drumm with Charles Kucyk, born June 2,
1923, WWII Navy seaman first class gunner

Mark, Mitchell, Lori, Maxwell Leibsla

HBO Honor Flight March 10–12, 2010

By the time the Honor Flight CAK "Special Flight" took place, the Honor Flight Network had "exploded nationally and (had) grown to include over 94 active hubs in 35 states," according to the program.

I first met PFC Arthur Cozza as a guardian on Honor Flight CAK on May 3, 2008. I signed up as a guardian to care for an oxygen-dependent veteran on the trip to see his WWII memorial and other memorials in Washington, DC. My husband volunteered too.

I learned about the special flight for Honor Flight CAK honoring veterans who fought in the Pacific theater during WWII. The trip's purpose, sponsored by HBO in partnership with American Airlines and Marriott Hotels & Resorts, was to invite Pacific WWII veterans to the premier of *The Pacific*, a ten-part miniseries based upon the true stories of WWII Marines who fought in the Pacific theater. The HBO miniseries, produced by Tom Hanks, Steven Spielberg, and Gary Goetzman, follows three Marines across the Pacific theater, PFC Arthur Cozza's comrades! Ack Ack had to be invited! Including Art proved to be a no-brainer. I made sure everyone at the event knew PFC Arthur A. Cozza fought with the men featured in the miniseries. He deserved every bit of fame he could get at that event. People did not disappoint Arthur and his family. Newspapers featured Arthur Cozza's story along with many photographs. Fans cheered Art and the other veterans on at The Chapel, Cleveland Hopkins Airport, Reagan National Airport, and at the Marriott Hotel. Television and newspaper reporters interviewed the Honor Flight veterans at airports and at the memorials. The veterans were welcomed home and escorted back to Akron-Canton Airport by an official procession of first-line responders. The masses of welcoming families, friends, military groups, motorcycle supporters, and others revitalized the veterans as they ended their three-day trip to Washington, DC. The hoopla amazed me. God blessed us all in a way which changed us all by participating in an unforgettable trip involving the Marines and other veterans who served in the Pacific theater. To God be the glory.

On March 10, 2010, thirty-five World War II veterans and twenty guardians waved goodbye to their families as they boarded the bus from The Chapel in Green, Ohio, on their way to Cleveland Hopkins Airport. Once at the airport, they were greeted by active-duty Marines, the press, and others. Banners hung everywhere honoring the veterans and the HBO premier event centering on the new miniseries, *The Pacific*. The veterans took part in a ceremony honoring their service during World War II. They soon boarded the American Airlines plane and soared off to Washington, DC. The greeting each veteran received in Washington, DC, brought forth many tears of joy as each veteran deplaned, received handshakes from active-duty military personnel, and settled into the airport while patriotic music played and cameras from the media flashed. News reporters interviewed the honored guests, and soon a press conference began adding to all of the pageantry.

The veterans relished in all the splendor, and they soon departed the airport by bus to the Marriott Gateway Hotel. After dropping off their bags, the bus brought the veterans to the Iwo Jima Memorial for photograph opportunities and interviews by active-duty Marines. This was Arthur Cozza's favorite memorial, if I remember correctly. He took pride in serving in WWII as a Marine.

Everyone boarded the bus again and the group arrived at Great American Steak & Buffet, in Falls Church, Virginia, for dinner. After bonding with other World War II veterans and guardians during dinner, the group arrived at Marriot Crystal Gateway Hotel, received instructions, and settled into their hotel rooms after picking up their goodie bags at the hotel.

March 11, 2010, started with breakfast at the hotel. Today was the World War II heroes' big day filled with the Korean Memorial, Vietnam Wall, and Lincoln Memorial visits culminating at the World War II Memorial. The ceremony began with a processional featuring the guests of honor that led to the area where they would all be honored at the memorial. Cameras lined the media area. Media representatives filled the grounds and interviewed the WWII heroes. The media filled the grounds of the World War II Memorial. The event honored the 250 distinguished WWII veterans from across the United States. I made sure Arthur Cozza was interviewed, stating that he was part of the Marines that were featured in *The Pacific*. Arthur beamed with happiness.

Earl Morse and Jeff Miller, cofounders of Honor Flight Network, participated in the event. I shouted with delight when I first encountered them on the airplane. I had not met them prior to this trip. As I boarded the airplane in Cleveland, I met two smiling handsome men at the back of the plane. They asked me what I thought about Honor Flight. Well, I didn't hesitate to gush out my admiration for the network and what an honor it was for me to serve. I told them all about Arthur Cozza and his role in this special event. After I finished with all my accolades, they revealed who they were to me. I almost fell over. What an honor to meet these amazingly generous, thoughtful, patriotic men. I made sure everyone knew who they were on the plane. I couldn't keep my discovery quiet. I tried to capture as many veterans as I could with my camera, introducing them to the founders of Honor Flight Network.

Steven Spielberg and Tom Hanks attended the event, along with the two main actors in *The Pacific*, Joseph Mazello, who played PFC Eugene Sledge and James Badge Dale, who played PFC Robert Leckie. Their presence honored the guests of honor, World War II veterans.

After all of the ceremonial events at the World War II Memorial, the veterans visited the Navy Memorial and the Air Force Memorial. To top off the day, the veterans enjoyed time visiting at the reception and dinner event at the Marriott. They chose whether they attended the viewing of *The Pacific* or *Casablanca*. Arthur chose to see *The Pacific*, and he appeared to handle the viewing well. I know others may have had difficulty with its content, and the organizers considered this fact in offering the other movie. The day proved to be beyond memorable.

March 12, 2010 started with breakfast and then room inspections. We loaded the bus once again and set off for the FDR
Memorial followed by the the Smithsonian National Air and Space
Museum with lunch at McDonald's. It was then time to depart from
Washington, DC, to Cleveland by airplane and then to The Chapel
in Green, Ohio, by bus. A big surprise awaited the veterans upon
arriving in Akron as they were greated and escorted by police with
flashing lights as the heroes they were and will be forever in our
hearts. I am writing this section of my book over the Independence
Day holiday, and my husband and I watched *The Pacific* in memory
of these courageous men.

An article in *The Repository* announcing the HBO miniseries Honor
Flight Trip featuring Arthur Cozza and Adone Calderone, WWII veterans

My patient, Richard Robinson, sent me this newspaper article which featured Arthur Cozza. Arthur was featured in *Morning Journal* on Sunday, April 4, 2010. The author, Matthew Schomer, wrote about Arthur's World War II experience. He used photographs I took on our HBO Honor Flight trip that I also feature in *Serving Heroes*.

Fred Rose, WWII veteran

PFC Arthur Cozza's family and others wave goodbye to
Arthur and the veterans as we left for the special HBO
Honor Flight three-day trip to Washington, DC.

Arthur Cozza, WWII Marine, Okinawa, and James B. Tedrick,
WWII Navy, Iwo Jima, autographing the American Airlines banner

American Airlines flight attendant, Dennis McKee, retired US Airways
Earl Morse, Honor Flight Network founder; Tom
Hutchinson, HF CAK board of directors member

The Washington, DC, news conference, arrival of Pacific
WWII veterans featuring the HBO miniseries, *The Pacific*

PFC Arthur Cozza being interviewed by a young Marine

HBO Honor Flight CAK

James B. Tedrick (upper photo) and Arthur Cozza (lower photo) being interviewed by young Marines

Two Marines connect.

Robert Marraccini, WWII veteran, with Paul Kully, guardian

Robert L. Davis found himself alone at the Vietnam Wall,
photograph taken by his son-in-law, Gene Whited.

Robert L. Davis wrote me in a letter penning, "I think (he) captured a never forgotten moment as I stared at the name of my neighbor's son who was killed in Vietnam early in the war. How sad. It's hard to believe that I had 'The Wall' all alone for a few precious moments. Such a great tribute to our fallen young 'Warriors.'"

Media attention galore

The Lincoln Memorial (in the background) honors the sixteenth United States President, Abraham Lincoln.

HBO The Pacific National Honor Flight. *The Pacific* was produced by Gary Goetzman, Steven Spielberg, and Tom Hanks and others.

Earl Morse and Jeff Miller, cofounders of Honor Flight Network and others at the Pacific National Honor Flight.

Two hundred fifty WWII veterans were invited to preview *The Pacific* HBO ministeries.

Plenty of attention… Arthur Cozza and Lloyd
Carpenter, and Pearl Harbor veteran

Marine attention

Pat Walker, Vietnam veteran; Joseph Keller and James Cardone, WWII veterans; Valere Turner; Lloyd Carpenter, WWII veteran; James Jackson with Paul Novak, WWII veteran

This is the Pacific pavilion, one of the two major military the-aters of World War II. The "Army, Navy, and Marine units fought a brutal island-hopping campaign across the Pacific against the Japanese," according to the Smucker's/Honor Flight brochure.

Two Marines greet one another, Edmund G. Farah and Arthur Cozza; other Marines being interviewed.

The two wreaths, wheat and oak, on each of the state pillars represents agriculture and industry, symbolizing those states and ter-ritories gave up their citizens, resources, and fruits of their labor to the cause of victory.

Calvin Double, Submarine veteran and Craig Double, guardian, son

Fred Dickenson

CPL Clifford Drumm and First Lieutenant Glen Royer

Lloyd Carpenter and Valere Turner, LPN

CPO Adone Calderone, Pearl Harbor survivor

USS *West Virginia* BB48 was sunk by eight torpedoes and four bombs. Adone swam to a lifeboat. All his clothes were blown off. He later went on to sink four Japanese carriers.

Dancers at the airport in Washington, DC, as part of the big send off for the veterans at one of the Honor Flights as they returned home

Troy Julian; Pat Walker, Vietnam Navy corpsman; Tom Hutchinson,
HF CAK board of directors member; Eric Hutchison; Jim Jackson

James Cardone, WWII veteran, Earl Morse,
Honor Flight Network founder

May 8, 2010 Trip
Mark: Robert Sobolewski, James Wise
Max: Robert Himes, John Shearer

This trip brought the Honor Flight CAK veterans to see their World War II Memorial along with FDR Memorial, Vietnam, Lincoln, Iwo Jima, and Korean memorials similarly to the other trips to Washington, DC. This trip differed, in that May 8, 2010 celebrated "victory in Europe Day at the National World War II Memorial."

The celebration included presentation of the wreaths to the freedom wall and to the Atlantic arch. Many groups participated and included the following: United States Congress, National Park Service, Friends of the National World War II Memorial, and Honor Flight. Fourth Infantry Division Association, Twenty-ninth Infantry Division Association, Eighty-second Airborne Division Association, 101st Airborne Division Association, 442nd Regimental Combat team; and Battle of the Bulge veterans Association also participated during the wreath presentations.

The Armed Forces color guard presented the Colors and the audience sang the national anthem, and the colors were retired. Speakers included Mr. John Piltzecker, superintendent, National Mall and Memorial Parks, LTG Claude "Mick" Kicklighter, USA retired, friends of the national World War II Memorial, Earl Morse and Jeff Miller, founders of Honor Flight, G. Evelyn Foote, USA retired, keynote speaker, and Senator Elizabeth Dole, keynote speaker. The United States Marine Corps Band played a musical tribute. The veteran visitors enjoyed the event.

As on other flights, the reception at the Akron Canton Airport brought tears of joy and huge smiles to the heroes' faces. The day proved to be another successful tribute to the veterans who served our country during World War II.

David Christein sent me a letter and a few photographs after this Honor Flight CAK trip. He wrote,

> Hello, thanks to you and all the people of Honor Flight for giving us a day that we will always know as the best. What a day. You made sure that we were taken care of and had a good day. As for me, you kept putting on sunscreen. I have had several bad cancers. Always had a smile. So, thanks again. I was all smiles when I arrived home at 11:00 pm. God Bless, Dave Christein.

I received a letter from William G. Carey in June of 2010. He apologized for taking so long to write due to being busy with construction projects occupying his day from 6:45 a.m. to 7:30 p.m. He wrote,

> I want to thank you Lori. The book you gave me is great and it is getting read by many people. I want to thank you again for being just who you are. You took time to help anyone at any time. I am sending you some pictures I think you will like. Now, for the most important part! Remember when you asked me to pray for you that God would open the right doors for you to be placed in the VA office where you could influence God's wisdom in their decisions? I have not missed one day praying for your request. I will keep praying until you tell me otherwise. With Love and Blessings, Bill Carey.

In January 2011, I received another letter from Mr. Carey. He wrote, "Dear Lori, I received your card before Christmas and we appreciated it very much. It sounds like our prayers were answered. When you make a move like you did and you are happy, Praise the

Lord He had something to do with it." He was heading to Hawaii and wrote, "Somebody has to go over there."

I recently spoke with Mr. Carey's daughter, Yvonne Carey Howell, by telephone. She gave me permission to write about her dad. William "Bill" G. Carey married Mitzi Jean Rowland on August 17, 1951. They had one daughter, Yvonne, two sons, David and Dana, and three grandchildren. Mitzi and Bill were married over sixty years. He modeled the man of faith that he was as a father in the lives of his children. His faith was real. He prayed for people without ceasing, and I certainly benefited from his prayers for me. He encouraged his children throughout their lives, telling them to "just do it," encouraging them to "stretch their wings."

Mr. Carey became a world class runner as a senior. He ran in South Africa, Tasmania, Australia, Japan, Quebec, Montreal, and other interesting places. He ran the Boston Marathon in his '70s. He traveled the United States running to qualify for races internationally. I have a feeling he was heading to Hawaii to run when he wrote to me back in 2011. He clocked in over fifty thousand miles over the twenty-one years he ran. He participated in five World Masters Games.

Bill Carey served on the USS *Midway* aircraft carrier during World War II. He served in the United States Navy for two years. Yvonne told me about a trip to San Francisco later in life when the family visited and toured the USS *Midway*. The family received an overwhelming welcome as they read "Welcome aboard, William G. Carey, plank owner." A plank owner is "an individual who was a member of the crew of a ship when that ship was placed in commission. Originally this term applied only to crewmember present at the ship's first commissioning," according to history.navy.mil. Yvonne shares they were "treated like God."

Mr. Carey was wounded on the USS *Midway* in a boiler room fire, and he inhaled smoke. He suffered living in the Akron area due to the rubber plants producing black smoke. He started making trips to Canada to breathe in the fresh Canadian air regularly.

I understand Bill was too young to get into the Navy, and his dad signed for him to go. He was a younger veteran, born on April 11, 1927. He enjoyed jitterbug dancing and invited all the ladies to dance with him. Once, when he was in Newport, Rhode Island, he had the opportunity to dance at one of the mansions. He danced all night long to big band music. His family later toured the memorable mansion. Bill and his friend were on the same Honor Flight trip. They enjoyed the unforgettable day, and Yvonne told me they were moved by the photographs I sent.

I admired Mr. Carey. I recognized his dedication to his savior, Jesus Christ, by the way he interacted with others. I honestly do not remember how we started talking. I simply remember how I felt talking with the amazing man of God. His smile warmed my heart. I tried to keep in touch; but as with others, life got in the way, which makes me sad if I think about it too long. I wanted to soak up veterans' histories at the time. I took notes when they shared their experiences which I had to find to tell their stories, even if in a brief line or two. Photographs of Mr. Carey and others bring back such wonderful memories of the Honor Flight trips. My family, coworkers, friends, and I received many blessings as we served these special veterans. I enjoyed learning more about Bill when I spoke to Yvonne recently. As with Mr. Carey, most of my veteran patients from the Honor Flights have passed. It comforts me to know that Mr. Carey is with Jesus in heaven, no doubt about it!

William Gene Carey enlistment photo

Year 1989 World Veterans Championships, Eugene, Oregon

The Carey Family, sixtieth wedding anniversary. In relation to William Carey: Yvonne Howell, daughter; Bob Howell, son-in-law, husband of Yvonne Howell; David Carey, son (in black shirt); Aaron Carey, grandson (son of Dana in striped shirt); Abbey Carey, granddaughter (daughter of Dana, in white top, longer hair); Dana Carey, son (in khaki shirt); Valerie Carey, daughter in law, wife of David Carey (in all white outfit). From left to right of the folks who are seated: Bill Carey, Mitzi Carey (Bill's wife).

James Wise, Robert Sobolewski, Mark Leibsla

The George Smith Family

Emerson Milner

John Shearer, Robert Hines, Max Leibsla

William Carey, Mark Leibsla (front left), and other guardians and veterans

Emerson Milner, Peter Kerr, Joe Hafer

Each of the gold stars to the right represent one hundred American military deaths. There are 4,048 stars. Do the math. There was one death out of every forty Americans who went to serve our country.

Veterans WTC3 William Carey, LCDR Lori Drumm

The Atlantic Pavilion in the background represents one of two major war theater locations. Navy ships transported Army and Marine personnel to fight in Northern Africa and Europe against the Germans and the Italians.

Coxswain 3C Thomas Haralson

David Christein and Lori Drumm, photo courtesy of David Christein

September 18, 2010, CAK Honor Flight

Mark and I received a thank-you card from Norman J. Fabick from Hartford, Ohio, at Christmastime. He apologized for waiting "so long to send my 'thank yous!'" He had been hospitalized twice for illness and obviously wrote to us when he felt better. He told us he "gave a small talk to (his) VFW#3521 on (his) trip and (he)gave Smucker all the credit for sponsoring this trip and all the time and money and all the employees who gave their time to act as Guardians. (He) read the fun facts from the booklet (they) got at the airport. 18 Vets over 90 years old, oldest 98. 10 female Vets, 30 Smucker Guardians." He ended his card, "Again I want to say a heartfelt thank you to Mark and Lori for all you did for us. The picture album you put together was just great. Again, thank you, Norman J. Fabick."

Patients of mine surprised me on this trip. Michele Hoffman, RN, accompanied her uncle, my patient, Francis Aowad. William Spatz, another patient, made me smile when I saw him at the airport. Staff Sergeant James Stevens delighted me too when I saw him grinning ear to ear. Paul Sprang joined us on this trip also. I remember buying him a spaghetti dinner at our neighborhood restaurant. It was great to see him on HF CAK.

Veterans S1C Edmund Scott, S2C Norman Fabic, George Gresh.

George Gresh was in France as part of the Air Corps. He made forty-three trips to Germany as an A20-gunner staff sergeant. He served from 1941 to 1945. Following WWII, George worked in the meat market for twenty-five years. He had four children, three boys and one girl.

I received a Christmas card from Bill Spatz that year stating, "Merry Christmas to you and your family. Thanks for September 18th and the pictures. You're a great Dr., keep up the good work. Bill Spatz." Glory to God!

Lori Drumm, William "Bill" Spatz, Jordan James, Albert Yeagley

S1C Edmund Scott and S2C Norman Fabick

Michele Hoffman, RN, with her uncle, Francis Aowad, Allen Rom

James Stevens, Valere Turner, LPN, Homer Slabaugh

Max eating a Crustible by Smucker's, William Bergemann

Sgt. James Stevens dances with a pretty girl.

George Gresh with his family

William Spatz and family

Francis Aowad and family

May 14, 2011, Honor Flight CAK trip, Ty Geiser and I are bus captains
Max: Olin Conrad
Mark: Ralph Clayton and Dwight Shaffer

I was able to enjoy Mark and Max on this trip along with my nursing coworkers, Mary Ann Noland, RN, and Valere Turner, LPN. Two of my clinic patients enjoyed being honored all day, and of course, I found myself in many pictures with Jack Senften and James Zeller. Other guardians who served on this flight served family members. Robert Sicker served Dario Sicker and Eugene Sicker. James Zeller's guardian was David Zeller. Joseph Tabellion's guardian was Kenneth Tabellion. Lyle Pohly's guardian was Lyle Pohly. Charles McDermott's guardian was Richard McDermott. Irin Musson Junior's guardian was John Musson. William Baker's guardian was Janice Baker. Ross Emery's guardian was Michael Emery. John Drennan's guardian was John Drennan. Andrew Rinaldi's guardian was Peter Rinaldi. World

War II veterans traveled together with another family member and included previously mentioned Dario and Eugene Sicker, Jack and Robert Haas, Harry and Robert Heath, Albert and Robert Schroeder, and Bruno and Clyde Stanga.

Honor Flight CAK guardians, bus captains, and our executive director served on this flight with family members. Valere Turner, LPN, brought along her husband, Rod Turner, and daughter, Kimberly Pierson, as guardians. Valerie Street Kinney served with her son, Kyle Kinney. Diane and Troy Julian served as the Yellow Squadron captains. Mark Leibsla, my husband, served as a guardian along with my stepson, Max Leibsla, the bagpiper.

This trip started out at the WWII Memorial, followed by visits to the Vietnam, Korean, and Lincoln Memorials, FDR Memorial, Iwo Jima Memorial, and Air Force Memorial. As was tradition, we sang "God Bless the USA" back to Reagan National Airport. As we entered the Akron Canton Airport, the veterans received a hearty welcome-home by the large crowd.

Lori Drumm, James Zeller, a patient of mine, David Zeller, son

Audrea Wynn, Jack Senften, a patient of mine,
with Sherry Wey in first class

Red, White, and Blue bus with Mary Ann Noland
smiling up front, a Canton VA nurse

Founder Earl Morse welcomes the HF CAK
WWII veterans and their guardians.

WWII Memorial: Robert, Dario, Eugene Sicker

Dwight Shaffer, Max Leibsla

The WWII Memorial honors the sixteen million who served in the armed forces during the war, four hundred thousand who died, and more than seventy million casualties.

Kimberly Pierson with Harry and Robert Heath

Dwight Shaffer with Senator Bob Dole, Olin Conrad to the right

Ralph Clayton, my patient, Lori Drumm at the Korean War Memorial

Red, White, and Blue bus at the Iwo Jima Memorial

The Turner family and their WWII veterans
enjoy the Air Force monument.

Ralph Clayton and Lori Drumm dancing at the airport

Jack Senften, my patient, receiving a kiss from one of the dancers

A welcome home by the Sicker Family

Another welcome home by a creative family!

May 19, 2012, Honor Flight CAK trip

Mark and I bonded with many veterans on this trip. I usually put together small photograph albums of the veterans we served during the Honor Flight CAK trip. We received a heartfelt card from Donald R. Draper from Cuyahoga Falls, Ohio, on June 23, 2012. Don wrote,

My dear friends Mark and Lori, You two never stop giving your LOVE and FRIENDSHIP. God had a hand in directing you guys to me on that great day I had. I truly wish I could see you both again!! As great a day it was for me as a veteran, you guys made it even greater with your love and care!!! God bless you both! The book is a great memento of that care and affection you showed. Call or come see me the next time you are close to Akron please! Again, Love to you, Don.

As I read Don's card nine years later, I am sad we did not visit him.

I received a letter from my patient and Honor Flight CAK veteran, Jack E. Lemke, from this trip on July 12, 2012. He wrote, "Dear Lori, it was a real nice surprise when I opened the memory photo packet. That was a real neat thing to do and really is something to keep with my other flight paperwork. At lunch, the other day with retired men from where I worked, I was telling them about the flight and how great it was. Your name came up, one of the men, Dan P., had been a patient of yours at the VA. He was glad to hear about you. He said that you were the best doctor he has ever had. My wife and I agree. *Absolutely,* his wife, Jane, added… Since my flight many of my friends have told me what a great thing you and your people have done. We agree you all do a fantastic job. Thanks for making this Vet proud. It was also nice seeing you again. My wife and I wish you the best. *We love you Lori, God bless us all,* Jane adds.

My cup overfloweth.
Jack Lemke included his thoughts about his welcome home in 1945.

It is a day I'll never forget. It starts on a troop train from New Mexico heading to the New Jersey coast to head overseas. The train stops at 3:00 or 4:00 a.m. in the morning. I am on that train. I look out the window. I can't believe it. We are sitting on the main street, Market Ave. in downtown Canton, my hometown. I walked out of the door and stood there thinking, "Gee, my mother and dad are only a couple minutes away from me." It started me thinking as I watched the city disappear as the train left Canton. If I come home ever from the service and it is by train, I'll get off the train and walk right up Market Ave. I dreamed of that day all through my two years away. It happened July 1945. I got off the train at 2:00 or 3:00 in the afternoon. Nobody there; just good old Market Ave. Like I had day-dreamed about, I walked to the Canton Engraving where my dad was at work. When he saw me for the first time in a year and a half, what a welcome. We headed for home, saw my mother waiting for a bus. I was driving. When she saw me, I'll never

forget her look… She came running to the car. A
good thing there were no other cars around. That
was a welcome that I dreamed.

I spoke with Frank Yarsa who met an Australian girl in 1945.
He wrote her a letter twenty years later without a reply. He wrote
her again thirty-five years later and received a reply. He waited fif-
ty-five years to hear from her, and at the time of the flight, they saw
each other every three months—blessings God gives us when we least
expect them.

Lori Drumm, Lori Hinderer, Karen Null, Ty
Geiser, Pat Walker, Jim Jackson

Mr. and Mrs. Jack Lemke (in wheelchair); daughter Cindy; Rachel Scruggs, guardian; Earl Taflan, veteran; and Lori Drumm

Excited faces…we were on our way to Washington, DC! Ralph Walter; Pam Overcasher, HF CAK board member and guardian; James Gall

Donald Draper, United States Navy, fireman first
class, and a photograph of his wife

Ivan Kitchen, veteran; Junior Miller, my patient, veteran, an electrician

Junior Miller and his daughter, Cheryl Haswell

Elizabeth Dole poses with the veterans at the WWII memorial.

James McDougal, Mark Leibsla, Donald Draper

Army Staff Sergeant Robert Schwartz at the Korean Memorial

Theodore Szendel, Lori Drumm, John Mrvica, my patient

James W. McDougal's dog tags and wife's photograph

Swinging to the big band music, Mark Leibsla and
Donald Draper, James McDougal, John Mrkvica

Heading home on United: Mark Leibsla,
James McDougal, Donald Draper

Welcome home, Robert McKinney! Thank
you for your service to our country!

Thank you, J.M. Smucker Company for sponsoring this trip!

Thank you, William "Bill" Carey and family, for welcoming
us home! (He was on the May 8, 2010, HF CAK trip.)
Mitzi Carey, Dana Carey, William Carey

My patient and his wife

Elmer Carpenter, WWII Marine veteran, with guardian, Sherry Wey

Welcome home, Donald Draper!

Welcome home, John Mrkvica!

Mission Accomplished Flight: September 22, 2012.

This HF CAK trip was sponsored by the J.M. Smucker Company. Paul Smucker, the grandson of the J.M. Smucker Company founder, served in the South Pacific aboard the USS *Cassin Young* (DD 793). He was a line officer on the destroyer. He endured kamikaze raids and rescued over 120 sailors from the destroyed Princeton carrier.

This trip completed the mission of Honor Flight CAK to take the Greatest Generation serving during WWII at home or overseas, to see Washington, DC, to see their memorial at no cost to them. Honor Flight CAK staff, directors, guardians, and contributors served over 1,100 WWII veterans from the area. Valerie Street Kinney served as executive director HF CAK, a fearless and tireless leader, motivator, and loving friend. Her two sons, Kyle and Ryan Kinney, Harry Donovan, Tom Hutchison, Valerie Street Kinney, Kathy Mossbarger, and Pam Overcasher served on the HF CAK board.

Many families donated in memory of those from the Greatest Generation. Donations were made in memory of Richard Bigham, May 8, 2010 flight, James Lange, HBO flight, Elsie Brooks, September 12, 2009 flight, Henry Seften (a patient of mine), and Wallace Lytle, September 20, 2008, flight.

My husband, Mark Leibsla, stepson and bagpiper, Maxwell Leibsla, and I all served veterans on this trip. I loved that we all had a job to do, and we all loved being part of such a wonderful organization. Honor Flight CAK appreciated us and so many of us who served became good friends. As I write this book and seek people's permission to include them in photographs, we reconnect and share Honor Flight memories. Yesterday, I interviewed Patrick Walker, my bus co-captain, a Vietnam War corpsman.

Patrick "Pat" Walker, born December 17, 1949, in Barnsville, Ohio, grew up in a household with two brothers and two sisters where they were taught to respect their elders and appreciate what those who went before you and respect the ones who got you here to begin with, especially those who served their country.

Like many others, Pat was drafted on his eighteenth birthday; but since he was still in high school, he was sent home to finish his high school education. We did not understand the Vietnam War at that point in time, and many Americans opposed the war; some deserted the United States. Internet did not exist in the 1960s and 1970s. Cell phones did not exist. Communication came through newspapers, radio, and television. Instantaneous access to events in other countries could not even be imagined at that time. When Pat was sent home, like others not thrilled about being drafted and sent to Vietnam, he thought joining the Navy would mean a ticket somewhere far away from the Vietnam War. Unfortunately, the Navy attached him to the Seventh Marines Second Division as a Navy corpsman in Vietnam. He was attached to H&S Company 27, a headquarters and service company, a company-sized military unit, found at the battalion level and higher in the United States Marine Corps. Pat became part of the infantry in Vietnam.

Pat Walker's introduction into the military shocked this young man. Trained as a machinist in high school, he was thrown into medical training he did not expect or imagine. He graduated high school on May 30, and by June 9, he raised his right hand and became part of the United States Navy. By August, he ended up at Naval Training Center San Diego. The trainees were ordered to pair up with a partner to practice starting IVs and giving shots. The leading nurse threw livers and oranges at the new corpsmen and instructed them to sew up livers and oranges which were in pieces. For a young eighteen-year-old expecting to work as a machinist, this new unimaginable lifestyle engulfed his thoughts and mind. He learned how to deliver babies. The learning curve exponentially skyrocketed. His knowledge base increased immensely and rapidly. No alternatives to this life existed. He trained to become a corpsman during the Vietnam War. About 10,000, Navy hospital corpsmen served with the Marines in Vietnam. About 645 corpsmen were killed, and over 3,000 were wounded in action. Pat would soon unknowingly lose one of his comrades, a corpsman in Vietnam.

Pat gave shots to recruits for about five months at Naval Training Center San Diego. He then trained at Camp Pendleton to become part of the Medic Marine Corps. He soon headed to Okinawa and ultimately landed in Da Nang, Vietnam. According to history.net, "Da Nang was the place where the first U.S. combat troops landed when the Marines came ashore in March 1965. By January 1968, it hosted high-level U.S. and South Vietnamese operations, including the headquarters of I Corps, the military zone encompassing South Vietnam's northern provinces."

According to vvmf.org (Vietnam Veterans Memorial Fund), medics and corpsmen provided trauma care on the battlefield, provided day-to-day prevention and treatment of disease, and treated a wide range of injuries and diseases. As part of my combat casualty care course, training for combat as a Navy physician, I watched indescribable videos from the Vietnam front line. The scenes were so horrific and overwhelming that I fainted twice during the videos which were meant to prepare us for war. The first Gulf War didn't last long, and I did not end up serving overseas. However, Pat served during wartime. What he witnessed and endured, I cannot imagine; but war became a day-to-day reality and job to him.

Pat Walker and the Marines landed in Da Nang, Vietnam, an extremely hot environment mixed with periods of excessive rain. After he and his comrades set up their quasit hut, his gunny sergeant announced they were going someplace, and "the fun began." Rockets sounded for an hour, and within that hour, Pat found himself addressing a shrapnel wound that tore open a Marine's left shoulder resulting in a shoulder looking like a "ham hock laid wide open." Four days later, they encountered their first firefight which was "not pretty" and frightened the unseasoned infantry. They soon became seasoned, trying to avoid any type of conscious fear that could let down their guard which could lead to mistakes according to Pat. In the bush, Pat described, there was "an awareness around you and your buddies 99 percent of the time." I asked him about sleeping, and he described one or two-hour naps and feeling like he had to sleep with one eye open, which of course, he did not do. Since he had to pay attention, sleep was not a good idea. Perhaps he could take advantage of quick pass outs, but there were no full night-sleeping arrangements. When in the rear, he slept better; but I don't think Pat spent much time in the rear. Banging noises startled him and the others, instantly bringing them to full consciousness. I don't think Pat or the others fighting the war slept much during their time in combat.

The food provided to the infantry during Vietnam began as C-Rations, food older than he was. Pat described C-Rations containing a slice of beef, mashed potatoes, ham slices, crackers, a piece of chocolate, peanut butter sometimes, cigarettes, and some type of fruit. "Peaches were the best." Food, water, ammunition, clothes, and other items were supplied to the troops by helicopter every four to five days.

Pat described one stretch of time, sixteen days, where rain prohibited replenishment of supplies to him and his comrades. The days were long, especially when encountering a sniper in a tree resulted in Pat running out of ammunition from shooting at the sniper in tree. Pat became annoyed as he explained trying to describe the situa-tion to a compensation and pension veterans benefits administration employee who obviously was not a combat veteran and had no clue what Pat endured in Vietnam. The employee did not understand why Pat would be firing into the tree. I would have been just as ignorant having not experienced combat; but Pat did not want to stir up nightmares, trigger more post-traumatic stress symptoms, or allow his anger to surface during encounters with others who could not relate to what he endured as a war veteran. As a result, Pat often avoided and still avoids situations that would elicit poor behavior.

They were always moving. They did two to three clicks a day, which I learned is a distance of one kilometer or 0.6214 miles, bor-dering on the rubber line of crossing into the prohibited territories of Laos and Cambodia. Pat's toughest memory appears to have occurred during an ambush where a close brother lost his life, another corps-man. They were close. Pat's biggest regret is not being able to get to the corpsman to help him. The enemy shot the corpsman in the knee. Training for extremity injuries entailed periods of tightening and loosening the tourniquet. Most likely, the corpsman went into shock during the loosening period, lost consciousness, and bled to death. By the time Pat arrived at the scene, the corpsman had been bagged up. "It was tough losing a brother. He was pinned down, shot in the knee, and bled to death." After that day, Pat chose not to get close to anyone stating, "Once you lose one, you try not to get attached to another. Guys went off the deep end (losing comrades)." There was no time for mourning in Vietnam. The corpsman died. He was put in a body bag and helicoptered away. The others went back to work. He shared, "Joe's gone. Here's Mike. It's the next day." Often the new person to arrive was a brand-new recruit without a clue and scared for the first three to four days. "Once climatized and into the groove routine of things, they had the same look in their eyes (like the rest of them)." They went onto the next day.

I wondered if Pat thought he would make it home, so I inquired. He told me they all thought they would eventually make it home. He said they all had a countdown calendar, and they knew about when they would be leaving within a two to three-week period of time. Pat served as a corpsman in Vietnam for thirteen months. He endured a serious case of malaria during his service, was medevacked to Da Nang (which infuriated him to have to leave his troops), improved, was sent for reacclimatization for four to five days, and eventually rejoined his troops.

Pat ended his Navy career as a corpsman stationed at Beeville Naval Air Station in Texas where "jet jockeys" trained. He joined a search and rescue team, picking up pilots who failed to do their job correctly, sometimes resulting loss of their lives. He described one pilot who made a "critically bad judgement call, fell asleep at the stick, and ran (his plane) into the ground." I believe it was in Texas where Pat lost a stripe or two responding to superiors who infuriated him with their delivery style. No war-seasoned corpsman liked being addressed as if he was twelve years old. Nor does any war-seasoned corpsman appreciate being berated, especially publicly. This disrespectful treatment changed Pat forever, along with the war.

I asked Pat what advice he would give to someone seeking his opinion about entering military service. He replied, "Yes, do it." He believes that everyone, ages eighteen to twenty-one, should serve two years in the military or other government agency. "Some kids have no clue what they are doing, no thought process." When young people, and I believe he included his young self, "are young, drunk, and dumb, it only leads to trouble." I agreed.

I asked Pat about what it was like for him to be part of Honor Flight CAK. He said, "It's the best thing I ever did for me...for veterans... There would have been ugliness [had he not been a part of Honor Flight trips]." He elaborated that talking with one older veteran, he learned that the WWII veteran's wife and daughter never knew about his WWII combat experience for fifty-three years. The daughter cleaned out her parents' home when they were moving into assisted living, and she discovered her father's shoebox filled with WWII memorabilia. The veteran's wife never knew her husband served in WWII.

The three-day special HBO *Honor Flight* proved to be difficult for Pat. The premier of *The Pacific* brought back too many war memories. In one scene of the miniseries premier, there was a look in the actor's eye that he had seen a thousand times "that you never want to see in a man's eyes." He also avoided The Wall on his first Honor Flight trip, sending his two veterans to see it on their own, meeting them "on the other side." Little did he know, the Vietnam Women's Memorial was "on the other side" and caught Pat off guard. On another Honor Flight trip, another guardian essentially "forced" Pat to visit The Wall. He didn't make it very far. He saw names he knew. One guide was giving a speech and encouraged Pat to find the location of the corpsman who died in the book containing location of Vietnam veterans who died. He found his brother's name on The Wall.

Honor Flight "made a hell of a difference in my life." He listed Val, Diane, Ty, Pam, Jim, me, Don, the physical therapist, Valere Turner, and more as all the people he appreciated. We laughed about one guardian who had to be hunted down on one flight after deserting his duty with a veteran. I guess we weren't all there for the right reasons.

I informed Pat that I am including many photographs in my book. I took so many photographs, and technology has changed over ten years. I shared that it is difficult locating the photographs, videos, CDs, DVDs, and old computers holding my precious memories from the past ten years after three moves to three different states. He told me he is not one for pictures, but Pat shared that he regrets not taking a picture with the only military friend from Texas days that he stayed in contact with during a visit to Hawaii a couple of years ago. He hopes to visit him again and have a photograph taken of them together.

Pat married Marsha in 1973. They are still married and have three children, two daughters and a son, and have five grandchildren. Long-term marriages are rare for Vietnam veterans. According to VA government statistics, "Approximately 38% of Vietnam veteran marriages failed within six months of the veteran's return from Southeast

Asia. Veterans are more than 60% more likely to separate or divorce than nonveterans." "There's an exceptionally high rate of divorce among active military and veterans due to the symptoms they've experienced during their service," according to Faith Lane, a VA clinical social worker and Warrior to Soul Mate facilitator on December 9, 2019. According to LawInfo Writer, reviewed by Ally Marshall, ESQ. on March 5, 2020 in an article titled "Why Is the Divorce Rate for Military So High?", "Multiple and extended military deployments can strain a marriage beyond repair. Besides separation from their loved ones and daily dangers, deployed service members face continued physical and mental health issues after they return home." As a physician working as a general medical officer in the Navy and family physician at the Veterans Health Administration (VA), I witnessed the suffering that divorce caused. I worked closely with mental health professionals on a daily basis treating active-duty military members, their families, and later veterans for post-traumatic stress disorder (PTSD), anxiety, depression, anger issues, homelessness, and legal concerns. Unfortunately, veterans have a much higher rate of suicide compared to the civilian population. I know firsthand of multiple situations where veterans committed suicide on VA grounds. These tragedies affected many people beyond the desperate veterans. I believe God blessed Pat's marriage to Marsha. Pat told me he has a difficult time developing close relationship; but there must be something about Marsha that enabled Pat to withstand the marital test of time. I see Pat on Facebook with his grandchildren, and the smile on his face tells me his heart can be opened wide by family. I believe Pat most likely bonded just fine with the new puppy, Cocoa, a cute little shih tzu, poodle mix.

Pat Walker currently "gives back" with other veterans on combat veteran group motorcycle rides. The group raises money for a charity, and as you may guess, this group supports Honor Flight, Inc. They raised about $8,000 during their first year of riding. Their ride for August 2021 had already raised $5,000 prior to the event. Pat shared, "Honor Flight helped me, so I am trying to give back." He reminded me that just like the high daily death rate of the World War

II veterans when we were on the flights, today the Vietnam veterans are dying daily at those high rates, more than the Korean veterans by far, due to the chemicals that were sprayed upon them. According to the US Department of Veterans Affairs (VA), Agent Orange "was a tactical herbicide the U.S. military used to clear leaves and vegetation for military operations mainly during the Vietnam War." New conditions, bladder cancer, hypothyroidism, and parkinsonism newly made the presumptive conditions caused by Agent Orange. Cancers caused by Agent Orange include chronic B-cell leukemia, Hodgkin's disease, multiple myeloma, non-Hodgkin's lymphoma, prostate cancer, respiratory cancer, including lung cancer, and some soft tissue sarcomas. Other diseases include amyloidosis, chloracne, diabetes mellitus type II, peripheral neuropathy, porphyria cutanea tarda, ischemic heart disease, and certain birth defects in children of Vietnam and Korea. Amyotrophic lateral sclerosis (ALS), also known as Lou Gehrig's Disease, is considered a service-connected disease but is not related to Agent Orange exposure. Some of the Korean veterans "who served along the demilitarized zone (DZM) in Korea during the Vietnam War now have an easier path to access health care and benefits," according to the VA. I certainly treated and served many patients with these diseases during my fifteen years at the VA. Pat presently receives services from the New Philadelphia Community-Based Outpatient Clinic (CBOC) which is part of the VA health-care system. I worked at this clinic when I first began to serve veterans as a VA employee in 2002. The clinic was state of the art as part of many efforts by the Department of Veterans Affairs to improve health care and provide the "best care anywhere" as described by author Phillip Longman.

While working at the VA, as I reflect, I failed to communicate well with some of the veterans. I regret that during my younger years, my inexperience and ill-placed passions interfered with empathetic communication with some of the veterans I served, especially those who were angry and spoke loudly. I remember being fearful at times when some veterans appeared to blame me for their difficulties with government encounters, especially VA encounters. My gut instinct often served me well; but at other times, I am certain fear took over for no reason. Hopefully, most of the time I listened to veterans' concerns and addressed them while offering preventive care. I developed amazing relationships with many of the veterans, along with their families when I served them as their primary care physician at the VA. Many veterans and family members kept in touch with me after I relocated to VA Central Iowa Health Care System, VA Northern Indiana Health Care System, and Deer Lodge Medical Center in Montana. God blessed me with amazing relationships during my medical career.

Mark served Charles Warfield on this September 22, 2012, trip to Washington, DC. Charlie wrote to us at Christmastime writing,

> Mark and Lori, thank you for the beautiful album and extra pictures. It was very nice on your part to do this for me. Barb and Cheri thought it was very nice you would do this for me. Everybody that has seen it thought it was very nice. I was very fortunate to have such nice guardians as you. I hope you enjoy your candy and nuts as you sit around the Christmas tree. God Bess you and stay well in the new year. As ever your guardian, Charlie.

Max cared for George Miller and played the bagpipes during the trip. I discovered a thank-you card from Sally Heestand, George Miller's daughter, after the trip. She penned, "The Leibsla Family, thank you so much for your thoughtfulness and kindness shown to my dad. He has talked nonstop since the trip of all the great people, places he saw and the appreciation shown by all for his service. You are very special people and once again, 'Thank you' for taking care of my dad!"

I spoke with Henry Kappel during the trip. He served as an Air Corps sergeant. He wrote two books about China, *Six Days to Maruta* and *The Tourist*. I plan to purchase and read these books. I just uncovered information I wrote about Henry Kappel on a business card during the trip.

This HF CAK veteran group, as with other groups, arrived at the Akron Canton Airport early, met their guardians, boarded the airplane, and ate breakfast on the way to Washington, DC. Upon arrival at Reagan International Airport, the veterans received an overwhelming welcome to the capital that never grows old to those of us who are fortunate enough to serve on multiple Honor Flight trips. To see the veterans' faces light up with surprise during the water cannon salute and then again beam with delight as the uniformed service members extend their hands to the veterans as they deboarded the aircraft brought tears of joy to my eyes and warmed my heart. Many people took time out of their busy days to greet the WWII heroes. None of the veterans expected a hero's welcome upon arrival to our nation's capital. These busy people displayed an enthusiastic greeting of admiration toward the veterans. As the sea of people parted, allowing the veterans to pass by, the people shouted well-wishes, thank you, and welcome as the veterans saluted and shook many extended hands offered by grateful Americans. Members of the greatest generation arrived to enjoy a day they would never forget.

The group made their way to the buses, boarded, and proceeded to the World War II Memorial to the Pacific theater area for a group photograph. Honor Flight CAK completed its mission to provide a trip for WWII veterans in the area to see their memorial free of charge. The labor of love that Valerie Street Kinney, board members, core HF CAK team, and other volunteers provided, made each flight a success. Harry Donavan, a HF CAK board member, served in WWII in the Navy. He was part of seven invasions. Pat Walker, bus captain, served as a corpsman in the Vietnam War. Valerie Street Kinney's son, Kyle Kinney, serves in the United States Air Force. Ryan Kinney served our country as part of the United States Navy and later the United States Marine Corps. Kyle and Cece Kinney have two children. Kyle Kinney made serving in the United States Navy his career choice.

Dolores Street, Kyle Kinney, Valerie Street Kinney, Ryan Kinney,
Karen Street Null at Ryan's graduation from boot camp

Ryan's first deployment took him to Afghanistan as a corpsman
with the Marines. Ryan later joined the Marines following his service
in the Navy. He was then stationed in San Diego at Marimar.

Kyle was deployed three times to Abu Dhabi. Kyles's first
deployment to Abu Dhabi took place at the same time as Ryan's
(his brother's) deployment. Kyle flew aboard E-3 airborne warning
and control system (AWACS) aircrafts. E-3 AWACS "carry out airborne surveillance and command, control and communication(C3)
functions for tactical and air defense forces," according to *Airforce
Technology*. The radar technology of the aircraft enables air and sea
target detection at the same time. The tactical role of the E-3 is to
"detect and track hostile aircraft operating at low altitudes over any
terrain, and can identify and control friendly aircraft in the same
airspace." Strategically, the E-3 can "detect, identify, track, and inter-
cept airborne threats."

The Honor Flight CAK group spent time at their World War II Memorial, soaking in the elaborate design. Don Millikin, a veteran and Honor Flight guardian eloquently penned,

> This is the World War II Memorial in Washington DC. As a society we disagree on many things, but I think the majority of us can agree that this war was a necessary war to combat evil and fascism in the world and veterans of all creeds and colors made enormous sacrifices to combat this evil. The memorial was dedicated in 2004—after many of our World War II veterans were too old to travel to see it on their own. Because of this, an organization called Honor Flight was founded to escort these veterans to Washington to see their memorial. Many chapters sprang up all over the country and I was privileged to participate in a half dozen of the flights to Washington with the Akron Canton chapter lead by dynamo, Valerie Kinney. She set the standard for organization, attentiveness and caring for these veterans.
>
> Being with these veterans at this memorial was something that touched the very core of my being. The memorial is set up in chronological order of battles and events that occurred in World War II with ½ of it dedicated to the European war and the other ½ to the Pacific war. Escorting a veteran at this Memorial was always emotional. On two occasions, veterans I escorted, broke down crying when they got to battles they participated in. On one of these occasions the man and I sat down and he told me about things that he did and saw that he had never shared with his wife or children or anyone else but his minis-

ter. He said there were even a few things he had never shared with his minister. He said he just needed to tell someone who would understand, another veteran because I wouldn't judge him. As he talked and sobbed, I sat there with my hand on his shoulder comforting him the best I could through my own tears. This man had been carrying these memories for over 60 years and he just wanted to tell somebody about them before he died.

I do not compare what myself or other current veterans have done and seen with anything on the scale that the men and women of WWII endured. But please remember we send young men and women off to wars where we ask them to do things that we've been telling them their whole lives are wrong and immoral. When they come home, they carry these things with them deep inside. I will not make comments on the righteousness or necessity of any current conflicts. I will say the politicians of both parties need to be very very cautious before they expend the national treasure that are our young men and women in any conflict. They need to make sure that it is absolutely necessary for the well-being of this country and world. When they do make that choice, they need to give these young men and women every bit of support that they can.

Following the emotional visit to the World War II Memorial, the group boarded the buses, ate their Arby's Market fresh sandwiches, and toured Washington, DC. The next stop, the Vietnam, Korean, and Lincoln Memorials where Smucker's Uncrustables were served at the concession stand area. I caught some leaders and guardians resting at the concession stand with the veterans with my camera.

The next memorial visits included the FDR Memorial, Iwo Jima Memorial, and Air Force Memorial. The honored veterans enjoyed all of the stops, and I enjoyed capturing them on film. After a long and enjoyable day at our nation's capital and war memorials, we sang "God Bless the USA" on the way back to Reagan National Airport for the last time. This song, written by Melvin Lee Greenwood, became a time-honored tradition for us to sing heading back to the airport.

> If tomorrow all the things were gone, I'd work for all my life. And I had to start again with just my children and my wife. And I'd thank my lucky stars to be livin' here today. Cause the flag still stand for freedom and they can't take that away [Chorus] And I'm proud to be an American. Where at least I know I'm free. And I won't forget the ones who died who gave that right to me. And I'll gladly stand up next to you and defend her still today. Cause there ain't no doubt I love this land, God Bless the USA.
>
> From the lakes of Minnesota, To the hills of Tennessee. Across the plains of Texas, from sea to shining sea. From Detroit down to Houston, And New York to L.A. Well, there's pride in every American heart, and it's time we stand and say. That I'm proud to be an American, where at least I know I'm free. And I won't forget the men who died, who gave that right to me. And I'll gladly stand up next to you and defend her still today. Cause there ain't no doubt I love this land, God Bless the USA.

I belted out the words, singing along with Lee Greenwood playing overhead. Others sang too. Everyone had the words to "God Bless the USA" on the back of their programs. I never tired of that song. I loved singing it more and more on the many flights I had the privilege to serve. Once at the airport, veterans received kisses by pretty girls dressed in fancy dresses from the 1940s, and others enjoyed dancing or watching the dancers, colorful in their festive suits and dresses. Dinner took place on board the airplane as the heroes headed back to Akron-Canton Airport. The tired group deplaned. The bagpiper warmed up his pipes and led the once tired group to the biggest welcome they ever received in their lives. Red, white, and blue balloons formed an archway into the airport reception area where hundreds of people gathered, waved American flags, shouted "thank you" and "welcome home," shook hands, hugged, kissed, and loved on the World War II veterans. Patriotic music played in the background by a band. Families and friends swarmed the veterans. Tears flowed. Some heroes were speechless, filled with indescribable emotion that overwhelmed them. The welcome surprised every veteran. The welcome home was long overdue.

It was difficult to say goodbye to friends who had become family to me. We accomplished our mission. The moment was bittersweet. I played a role in many of my veteran patients' participation on the HF CAK flights. I told all of my patients about the opportunity. I enjoyed seeing them on flights, and I welcomed them home at the airport on other occasions. The joy on their loved ones' faces remains implanted in my memory and in my heart. God blessed me. I pray I served these heroes as Jesus would have me do. There is no greater servant to model than our Lord, Jesus Christ. To God be the glory!

Charles Warfield with family

Donald Scott, my patient from Canton VA

Max Leibsla with George Miller arriving at the airport in Washington, DC

Mission Accomplished! World War II Memorial

Back row: Max and Mark Leibsla with Reverend Willie Smith
Front Row: Charles Warfield

Elizabeth Dole greets George Miller with Max Leibsla, and
Charles Warfield waits for his turn to greet the senator's wife.

Mark Leibsla with Charles Warfield who was happy to have a camera

Waiting in line for food, veterans, and the statues. I
had fun posing the veterans for photographs.

Valere Turner with Eugene Kay, Max Leibsla with George Miller,
Mark Leibsla with Charles Warfield at the FDR Memorial

US Navy S1C Ralph Cooper with a pretty girl lipstick kiss

James "Jimmy" Stevens, my patient, greets us at CAK
Airport. Jimmy was on a previous HF CAK trip.
A grand welcome home and CAK Airport

Reverend Willie Smith with his wife of sixty-three years,
Virginia and others welcoming him home

Reverend Smith served in WWII and Korea. He later worked at BF Goodrich Chemical Plant and retired in 1985 after thirty-eight years of service to the company. He was the associate pastor at Grace Baptist Church for forty-eight years. Max, Mark, and I met Reverend Smith at Grace Baptist. He witnessed to Max, which led to Max accepting Jesus as his Lord and Savior.

HBO WWII Honor Flight veteran, Paul Novak, is there to greet us!

My patient, Donald Scott, with his daughter

Thank you J.M. Smucker Company for making this trip possible. Thank you for the goodie bags too!

CHAPTER 5

PFC ARTHUR "ACK ACK" COZZA

The Pacific

I interviewed Art Cozza at his home in East Palestine, Ohio, on July 20. 2008. My husband and I enjoyed the opportunity to visit with Art, his wife, and his family. Art joined the Marines on December 6, 1944, and served his country until October 29, 1946. Assigned to K35, K Company, Third Battalion, Fifth Marine Regime, First Marine Division as a Browning Automatic Rifleman, he left Parris Island, Camp Lejeune, behind as he headed to Norfolk, then Panama Canal, Hawaii, and ultimately Okinawa, Japan.

PFC Art Cozza fought during WWII, as one of 250 men replacing the original 235 men assigned to the fight the war in Okinawa, Japan. The only training PFC Cozza received was on the job training, also known as combat. Only 26 men of the original 235 men survived. Art was one of 26 men who survived from his group of 250 men, First Marine Division, who replaced the original Marines assigned to the island. Later, only nine to eleven Marines were left from Art's platoon, then eight. Art referred to a comrade, RV Burton, who wrote the book with Bill Marvel, *Islands of the Damned: A Marine at War in the Pacific* and his experience in Okinawa as a combat Marine along with PFC Art Cozza. Art continued his story, stating twenty replacements arrived. They lost 22 out of 30 tanks at Kunishi Ridge. He described the caves under the ridge filled with Japanese fighters. One hundred men would go up to fight, and only fifty would return. Then there was the next ridge to battle.

I asked Art what he would like to share with future generations. He started out addressing sea rations, food. He jokingly described a fellow Marine who would swap his sea rations for spaghetti, laughed out loud stating, "He sure loved spaghetti." Then his mood changed.

Their part of the island became littered with dead Japanese soldiers which brought disease. The American men tried to bury the dead, although this task was not part of their assigned duties, which consisted of covering them with sugarcane. The dead had bloated legs and were covered with maggots. When the Marines pulled them to bury them, their legs came off like chicken bones. Art, an eighteen-year-old Marine, experienced the casualties of war filled with grotesque visual realities incorporated with the indescribable stench of decaying bodies.

Art brought up sea rations again. They only received two cans daily, and once maggots filled his smashed cans, he did not eat that day.

The men patrolled on twenty-four-hour watches. Often, Japanese soldiers could be seen in close proximity. Other times, the Japanese hid in caves and the Marines constantly surveyed territory to their rear. Art became emotional as he described a sniper that killed a special Marine, Shorty Downs, who had four children. Art would have preferred it had been him at the time. The interview grew silent.

Art described foxholes and grenades landing in areas meant to protect them but instead killed men. A seventeen-year-old Marine accidentally killed a friend playing with a gun, was court-martialed, and eventually committed suicide after the war. The men climbed cliffs to visualize the war's front line. They saw a Japanese soldier in the road, flat as a pancake, from tanks running him over multiple times. Art begged another Marine not to light a cigarette because the light would bring on gunfire. As expected, the ignorant Marine lit his cigarette, and all hell broke loose. There was machine gunfire everywhere. As they approached the Army line, Art viewed what he thought was a dozen American tanks, knocked out and still smoking. He refers to R. V. Burgin's book and stated, "We lost twenty-two out of thirty tanks that day, one of the biggest battles at Kunishi Ridge." The Japanese artillery destroyed the tanks.

While waiting behind the lines in pickups ready to attack the Japanese at the break of dawn, Art's comrade, Harry Bender from Hawaii, was hit in the back of the neck with a bullet. Without the luxury of time to process this incident, the Marines climbed a hundred-foot ridge, desperately grasping onto trees and rocks. Soldiers who followed below, ducked from falling rocks; and in one instant, a Marine called Mose from Waco Texas, pinned by fallen rock, "had his nose up a Jap's rear end and could not raise his head." Art, on the other hand, sweated profusely affecting his vision from salty sweat filling his eyes. A sniper targeted three of the accompanying Marines and successfully ended their lives.

Art described himself as being a fast runner and escaped death when a sniper hit the back of his pack. At another location, the Marines hid behind ten-to-twelve-foot boulders facing the side of the ridge. Two Japanese officers, spotted by Art, walked in front of the two Marines, Art and Mose. Art caught Mose's attention, and after two quick bursts, Mose got them. Art's admiration for Mose's rifle skills became evident.

On another day, the Marines saw an American jeep speeding toward them, kicking up lots of dust with a trailer filled with rockets. Three Marines fired off the rockets, but they fell short of the enemy target into friendly lines. At a 1991 Marine reunion, Art learned from his buddy, Ski, forty-six years later that a friendly rocket hit Ski, sending him skyrocketing into the air fifteen to twenty feet resulting in a serious concussion. Two other Marines died from the friendly rocket fire.

A Japanese sniper took off the lieutenant's ear spraying blood onto Art. Harold Weeks, burned on the cheek for phosphorus, received a Purple Heart. Art had phosphorus burns on his face, hands, and fingertips, but no Purple Heart. Art hurt his back getting the lieutenant off the ridge. He and four other Marines carried their leader across two sugar cane fields. This effort left Art crippled and unable to continue with the group. Art hid in the field until he recovered enough to press on, and he joined his division on another ridge, the last ridge.

While close to the ocean with Japanese occupation, with only two-man foxholes, rocks only a foot high, and a thicket to conceal the nine to eleven Marines left from Art's platoon due to the terrain covered with solid rock, the men took turns sleeping. Art's turn to sleep finally arrived. As he squeezed in undercover as much as was feasibly possible, a sharp rock in his back made sleeping difficult; but the exhausted Marine slept. When Art was sound asleep, a thunderous explosion startled the Marine to full awareness, and Art grabbed his rifle from its protective location across his body. A machine gun riddled bullets. A hand grenade landed near Art and bounced back off the thicket landing at Art's feet. Something landed in his finger. He wrapped his bleeding finger with a hanky, turned around, and saw shrapnel in a tree where his head once slumbered. The piece of shrapnel missed Art's nose and helmet, landing in the tree sparing Art's life. Shorty Downs died that night from the sniper, leaving a widow and four children.

As the Marines looked over the cliff, they spotted a two-year-old Japanese boy wailing in an open field. The men learned that this was a trap by the Japanese to bring American soldiers out from hiding and into the open to ambush them. Sadly, the Japanese soldiers were thought to have killed the young boy's family, using him to ambush the enemy. Although difficult not to provide aid to the little boy, the men knew they would have been wiped out. There were only eight Marines left out of 250 men at that time. Four survived.

At one point, a Marine with an Irish accent picked up a Japanese prisoner with a gangrenous leg. He searched the prisoner, but he failed to examine the bad leg. As they turned the prisoner over to the Army, the prisoner was hit in the back of the head by a Marine, died, and fell backward. The prisoner was holding a grenade. The group did not know if the prisoner meant to toss the grenade at them or if he planned to blow himself up with the grenade, another near miss.

Art attempted to visit the Irish Marine later in life. Unfortunately, his war buddy found himself in jail. He served as the inside man, part of a Brinks armored car robbery in New York. Art's injury to his finger from the shrapnel wound festered and resulted in significant cellulitis, a deep tissue infection, that traveled up his arm. He said, "I was an eighteen-year-old kid, and I didn't know how to take care of it." With the aid of a corpsman, the abscesses were lanced, and Art's body healed.

The men did not bathe for months. Jungle rot and ice-cold showers, when available, left the Marines dreaming to go home. Art wrote home to his mother, and much of the letter was censored. He eventually was able to rest at a camp following a leg injury and serious skin boils. Art learned his close friend was almost killed on Kunishi Ridge when a sniper hit his helmet. This friend, Depiner, from Grand Rapids, Michigan, went on to study at UCLA, sold playgrounds to cities, and became a multimillionaire. Art visited his friend later in life as a truck driver. Art first located Depiner's mother, and he asked her if she had a son in the Marines who went to Okinawa. She said, "Yes." He asked if he came home with two bullets in his helmet. She said, "Yes!" Art learned Depiner went to California and became a successful businessman that day.

While enjoying his first bath in months, which proved unenjoyable due to the ice-cold water, Art stepped on coral or shrapnel, splitting his big toe wide open. A Japanese enemy located across the field was spotted, and all Art could do was wrap his toe with writing paper provided by the Red Cross and take cover.

As the Marines approached a rest area up north, Art rode shotgun in the back of the truck. The truck passed an American hospital, and as Art saluted the hospital, chills ran up and down his back with feelings of American pride. At the outpost, a skeleton of a Japanese soldier became visible. A tank off the road and to Art's left attracted his attention just as a buddy yelled, "Limb!" The warning came too late. The limb dragged Art into its branches like a "strainer" in a river and bloodied the Marine's body from knee to hip. Again, there was no time to see a corpsman. Art's body healed over time.

If you do not believe in God, think again. While serving in Okinawa, Art received a gift that only God could pull off. One day, while sitting in his tent speaking to a buddy, Art saw a Marine walking down the road with a big smile on his face. He did not recognize the Marine in the distance. The Marine walked up to Art's tent, invading his personal space, and Art yelled, "Go away!" Art looked up again. "It was my brother!" Art and his older brother by seven years, Frank, who joined the Marine Air Corp in 1942, were stationed in the same area in Okinawa, Japan! Frank could not believe Art survived the battles of Okinawa. Frank learned about the high casualty rate of the First Division.

Frank Cozza joined the Marines in 1942 at the age of twenty-two. He scolded Art for joining the Marines but at the same time expressed gratitude to see Art still in one piece. Art did not disclose his injuries to his brother.

The following weekend, Art tried to visit his brother on the south end of the island, about forty to fifty miles away by hitchhiking. As he held out his thumb anticipating a ride, a lieutenant picked him up and escorted Art back to his base because Art did not have a pass. Art tried this stunt again only to be picked up by an officer who brought him back to base. By the third week, Art found a way to get a pass and successfully arrived at Frank's location.

Art and his company enjoyed sea rations daily in Okinawa, some of which were maggot-infested and inedible. Sea rations are also very constipating and not full of flavor which is how hot sauce became so popular. Art attempted to visit his brother who enjoyed showers and better food such as steak, big pies, and hot beer (which Art learned to appreciate because ice was nowhere to be found). Marines were not the best fed, and Art reflected the food situation concluding, "Officers were probably stealing our food." The Army camps, on the other hand, had beer galore down the road. At one opportune moment, the Marines approached an army guard, stating they were taking over guard duty for them. The Marines loaded up their truck with provisions and later wondered what happened to the Army private who left his post. The Marines enjoyed some fun in a place surrounded by death and destruction.

At one point, Art was on a ship in Buckner Bay during a typhoon. As the typhoon with 175 to over 200 mile per hour winds circled the island for two or three days, everyone on board became seasick. Enduring fifty-to-sixty-foot waves, the rutter would rise in midair, shaking the ship only to crash down onto the water. Cruisers would disappear underwater and surface spilling water covering the deck back into the ocean below. To add insult to injury, Art's ship nearly capsized, and they saw their sister ship hit a mine with only an outcome filled with tragedy resulting. He spent his nineteenth birthday on the island shortly after the typhoon lost its power.

On August 14, 1945, World War II ended, and Art soon left Okinawa. Art finished his service as a combat veteran during WWII in Peiping (Beijing), China. Following a smaller ship voyage, time in tents, and a train ride, Art and his platoon landed in Peiping. The Marines feared being ambushed but expressed sighs of relief when Japanese officers saluted the Americans. The platoon paraded down the main street of Peiping. What seemed like millions of Chinese lined the street, waving American flags in celebration. The Chinese were liberated from Japanese control. Arthur Cozza enjoyed his last service months from September to August of the following year in northern China, often frequenting Chinese restaurants.

Arthur Cozza married Marion Mable "Midge" Cozza after his return from World War II. Arthur and Midge raised nine children: Richard, John, Dixie, Debbie, James, Randy, Vicki, Robert, and Dan. At the time of the interview, Art and Midge enjoyed their nine children, eighteen grandkids, and nine great-grandchildren. We have kept in contact through the years. Many of us are friends on Facebook.

Japanese flag. Top left to right: Rose, Feldman, Moses.
Bottom: Siebert, Weeks; Okinawa, South end of the island,
June 24, 1945.Photograph courtesy of Arthur Cozza.

Cecil Fitzsimmons (friend from school), Arthur Cozza, Condon
Photographs courtesy of Arthur Cozza

Courtesy of Arthur Cozza

A train ride to China, photo courtesy of PFC Arthur Cozza.
Off of the train in China. Arthur Cozza is on the far
right, profiled, hands in his pockets, dark hair.

Reunion Photos. Arthur Cozza has a patch on his eye.

Arthur Cozza's WWII memorabilia

Arthur showing me his uniform

CHAPTER 6

FRANK BENNETT, LEYTE GULF, GAMBIER BAY

Interviewed April 5, 2005

Frank Bennett was born on June 6, 1926. He told me he had a great life as a child. His mother and father were good parents to him and his two brothers. He attended Cambridge High School. He received high school credits for enlisting in the war and headed off to boot camp, Treasure Island, California, and ended up overseas. Both of his brothers served during WWII. One brother served in the South Pacific and survived. His other brother served stateside.

Abroad, Frank served on an aircraft carrier in southern Australia. His job entailed getting airplanes off of the carrier by putting them into position. As part of the Seaman Air Division, he and his crew headed off into combat. They engaged in several invasions. They encountered the Japanese Air Force and shot down several Japanese planes that attacked American ships. The Leyte Gulf invasion, known to be the one of the, if not the, greatest Navy invasion of WWII, became the site that challenged the USS *Gambier Bay* sailors and Japanese troops. During the main invasion, the Japanese Navy blocked off the gulf to the American aircraft carriers. The Japanese fired on the USS *Gambier Bay* carrier and sunk the carrier that carried Frank and his comrades. The captain announced, "Abandon ship!" The crew did just that. They abandoned the USS *Gambier Bay* aircraft carrier as it was sinking.

Frank initially had nothing to hang onto, and he swam out to some debris from the ship. He noticed two lifeboats off in the water; but they were filled with sailors. Frank held onto whatever he could. He had a jacket that soon became water-soaked and did not last long. For two long hot sweltering days and two long frigidly cold nights, Frank floated in shark-infested water. During the day, the visible sharks swarmed around him as he floated, and he tried to stay quiet to avoid attracting attention by the deadly blood-thirsty sharks. He worried all day as he watched the sharks encircle him. At night, he could not see the sharks; but he knew they were there. He shook and trembled from the cold during the long endless nights.

During the day, Frank spotted other guys who huddled in small groups or as individuals as they waited to be rescued. Frank stayed by himself, mostly holding onto flight deck wooden debris that floated as his legs dangled into the water. He stated, "There was nothing you could do." Then far away, Frank spotted a ship, and he wondered if it was a Japanese or American ship. He knew he was floating in enemy waters, but he swam toward the ship.

With help from the ship's crew, his battered body was hoisted up on the ship's deck, an American patrol craft. The patrol craft ship started pitching and rolling. Frank, weakened from being battered, cut, and bruised, could not stand upon the deck, move, or speak. Frank could not say his name, and he had lost his dog tags at sea. He remembers that he knew what was going on at the time; but he was too weak to respond. He felt lucky to be rescued. The crew rescued other stranded Americans that day as they pitched up and down in the waves.

Frank recalls being thirsty and hungry prior to his rescue, but there was nothing he could do about his situation at the time. He thought he could see land in the horizon at times along with mountains, but he floated too far away to attempt swimming toward the land. His face burned up from the sun. He became unrecognizable. The cold nights and the shivering haunted him.

The patrol craft brought the rescued seamen to the hospital ship, a luxury liner converted to a hospital ship. He saw other friends on the ship, and he smiled remembering them. The hospital ship docked in San Francisco, and Frank arrived at Oakland VA Hospital. Several friends, who were heading home for thirty-day survival leave, visited Frank at the VA hospital. Sadly, Frank, too beat up to head for home on a three-day coal train ride, remained in the hospital. After the Oakland VA stay, he relocated to a San Jose convalescent home. This former resort housed Frank and other recovering war veterans.

Frank contacted his family during his recovery time. He could not report what happened to him at sea. The sinking of the USS *Gambier Bay* shortly reached the newspapers, and his family became aware of the situation. Frank comforted his mother stating, he was all right and she should not worry. His mother had a bad heart, and Frank tried to console her. Eventually, Frank's wounds healed enough for him to endure the three-day train ride home to Cambridge, Ohio, for his thirty-day survival leave. He ended up back at a convalescent hospital for several more months until he was discharged from the Navy.

Frank told me he wanted to go back to the war; but he knew he physically was not doing well. He gave up his dream to become a fighter pilot. He discharged from the Navy, and he stayed at the VA hospital in Pittsburg, Pennsylvania, following an ambulance ride due to gastric illness from swallowing too much saltwater. This illness became a lifelong illness.

Frank's adjustment to civilian life after the war proved to be rough. His mother suffered a heart attack, and his father cared for his family. Frank smiled as he told me of his first train ride home to see his family. His mother smiled, and Frank felt great. After all, he was the youngest in the family, and he was finally home sweet home. His brother served in New Guinea at that time.

I asked Frank where he was when WWII ended. He said, "In my garage, working on my car." Glad the war was over, life continued. He never married. Veteran associations enabled Frank to keep in touch with comrades over the years. The year I interviewed Frank, he planned to attend a reunion. Frank sent for copies of reports about the USS *Gambier Bay* on television. He watched the tapes and noted that the Japanese had pictures of American ships. Japanese battleships closed in on American ships and circled them. He ended by telling me it (war) was scary, but they were all just doing their jobs, trying to get planes into the air."

Dr. Lori Drumm and Frank Bennett, Canton
Community Outpatient Clinic

Frank gave me the book *The Men of the Gambier Bay* by Edwin P. Hoyt, which highlighted Frank's aircraft carrier.

Admiral Thomas H. Moorer (USN, retired) wrote in the chapter titled "The Rescue,"

> Lieutenant Buderus, one of the CIC officers who had escaped just before the ship went down, had been injured and was bleeding from several wounds. He was told to stay on a raft but as morning came, Buderus felt he should take his turn in the water and he came down. Captain

Vieweg and Commander Ballinger ordered the rations opened again, and this morning the men had malted milk tablet and another bite of biscuit. Some could not wallow because their throats were so dry. Buderus was in the water when he got his rations, and he ate them. He was around the corner of the raft from Yeoman Hammond, and Hammond could see his white skivvy shorts. Buderus suddenly let out a yell. "A big fish," he shouted. Then he started screaming. The men in the raft above grabbed him and pulled him in. He was bleeding badly, and his entire buttocks had been ripped off. He had bad bites on his back and legs. He was half unconscious. There was nothing that could be done for him. The damage was too severe to remedy. He lingered for a few hours and died.

The men saw the shark that killed Buderus, and many other sharks encircled many rafts. The shark-infested waters were difficult to navigate and survive. The author describes many men becoming sick from drinking sea water, just as Frank did, resulting in short-term and sometimes lifelong illness. Others waiting to be rescued became delirious and visualized mirages.

CHAPTER 7

DOUGLAS "DOUG" BRYANT, THE NEW ENGLAND PACIFIC HBO HONOR FLIGHT TOUR

I flew on CAK Honor Flight as a bus captain and flight doctor to fly World War II veterans to see their memorial in Washington, DC. To my delight, I met an eighty-three-year-old submarine veteran from WWII who served twenty-five years in the Navy. A Navy veteran myself who served at Groton Submarine Base in Groton, Connecticut, it was delightful to cross paths with this special person. He penned, "It was especially rewarding for me to talk to you about the submarine base Groton, Conn. 'We have much in common.'" What a thrill for me!

On April 9, Doug sent me a photograph of us taken on March 11, 2010, at the WWII memorial. He wrote down his service history for me. He asked me to share his story with young men and women, "what the Navy did for me."

In August of 1943, Douglas Bryant joined the Navy on his seventeenth birthday without a high school education. He attended boot camp engineman school and went on to submarine school in

Groton, Connecticut. From 1944 to 1946, Doug served on the Submarine Sea Dog SS401 in the Pacific. They sank ten ships and received a few depth charges. A depth charge is an anti-submarine warfare (ASW) weapon which is dropped in the water near a submarine, detonated, and subjects the submarine to a powerful and destructive hydraulic shock to destroy the vessel.

In 1946, Doug served on the Submarine Spinax SS489. In 1947, he attended deep sea diving school and served as a 1/C diver (hard hat) for three years. WWII divers donned diving gear that typically consisted of wearing thirty-five-pound shoes, a thirty-pound dive belt, a twenty-five-pound dive helmet, and a one-hundred-pound dive suit. Divers had to kneel in the water, not lean, or otherwise, the suit would tip them over.

Doug earned his high school GED serving on the Submarine Sea Owl SS405 for five years beginning in 1950. In 1955, he was assigned to the Submarine Escape Training Tank as an instructor in scuba and submarine escape. From 1958 to 1967, Doug Bryant served on two other submarines and retired in 1967 as a senior chief engineman E8. He ends his letter to me stating, "Honor Flight New England, HBO, Tom Hanks 'Pacific' was one of the greatest things of my life. Thank you for being part of this. Doug."

Doug Bryant, WWII submarine veteran with Lori Drumm, Navy veteran

CHAPTER 8

JAMES B. TEDRICK

To his children, James and Joy, a chronical narrative of his Navy career April 26, 1943 to March 6, 1946, including the Battle of Iwo Jima.

James B. Tedrick entered the service on April 26, 1943, at Hartville Stark County, Ohio. He trained at boot camp naval training station, Great Lakes, Illinois. James trained at a diesel engine training school Co. 24 Navy Pier in Chicago, and his rank changed from A/S apprentice seaman to F 3/C fireman third class. He advanced in his diesel training to MOMM 2/C motor machinist mate second class petty officer. His future experiences and training in Miami, Florida, and San Diego, California, led to him being groomed to be part of GRO-PAC-11 Code Name Ground Pacific for the invasion of Iwo Jima.

James arrived at Coronado Navy Base, San Diego, California, and worked on the GM Gray Marine two-cycle series diesels in a camp consisting of tents sitting on sand. Avoiding sand scorpions became challenging. He moved on to San Luis Obispo and San Bernardino before boarding the USS *Saratoga*, the largest aircraft carrier in the US Navy with a Hawaiian island, Pearl Harbor destination as his first sea experience. His journey continued on a Navy cargo transport ship to the Marshall Islands and later as part of many AKA transport ships where he experienced true hunger when the ship's food supply diminished.

After docking in Saipan and boarding the USS *Belle Grove* LSD which took the crew to Iwo Jima for the February 19, 1945, landing just two weeks prior to the initial invasion, their mission was to take the island in three to ten days but ended up taking over thirty days with a very heavy cost of lives. Marines in the Third, Fourth, and Fifth Division suffered greatly. The island was under bombardment continuously. Battleships lined the sea, and "their sixteen-inch guns sounded like thunder a short time after the flash of firing." Warships, destroyers, and other vessels shelled the island with rockets and other artillery continuously. As James stood on top of the LSD, his legs shook uncontrollably. Afterward, he overcame fear.

James transferred from the USS *Belle Grove* LSD (landing ships dock) to LSM (landing ships medium), a 480-foot dock which enabled damaged ships to dock for repairs. The Japanese wired the coast to damage ships. The kamikaze Japanese fighters fastened explosives to their bodies, swam out to ships at bay, climbed up the anchors, and damaged ships.

Most notably for historians, while James worked on a disabled LCM, a bomb fifty feet long, close to the beach and off the coast at the foot of Mount Suribachi, he viewed the first famous flag raising on Iwo Jima which was raised again within the ten to fifteen minutes for the photographer to capture the event.

Following encampment on land, James served on the USS *Agenor*, a repair ship, LST (landing ship tank) converted to a diesel engine repair station. He experienced typhoons which tossed and twisted the ships, including one top-deck experience consisting of a great chance of being washed overboard. He wore two life jackets and rode eighty to one hundred feet high swells hanging on for dear life. His next stop was Saipan for a second visit. When the war ended August 14, 1945, soldiers were transported home based upon points earned in service. On a cargo ship, James traveled from Saipan to San Francisco. He then rode a train back home to Canton, Ohio, proudly wearing his first-class motor machinist mate rating and citations issued at that time.

Photo from James B. Tedrick's chronological narrative
of his Navy career to his children, James and Joy

James B. Tedrick, Iwo Jima veteran being interviewed by a Marine

CHAPTER 9

PAUL MASALKO

The Army drafted Paul Masalko, born January 16, 1920, in Mount Carmel, Pennsylvania, on October 20, 1941, and he served until December 17, 1945. Mount Carmel is in the Coal heritage Region of Central Pennsylvania. Paul attended basic training at Camp Wheeler, Georgia, served in Fort Leonard Wood, Missouri, trained at Camp Young, California Desert Training under General Patton, and then set off to Hawaii, New Guinea, and the Philippines during WWII.

I interviewed Paul on June 20, 2008. He proudly shared a diploma he received after crossing the equator titled "Ruler of the Raging Man" which was signed by his friends. This is a line-crossing ceremony that took place for WWII sailors who cross the equator for the first time. Other sailors, who crossed the equator previously, induct the new sailors into a fraternity of seasoned sailors. Paul proudly displayed his diploma. He never saw his friends who signed his diploma again.

Paul shared meeting up with a frontline WWII medic again after the war working in a factory. He also reunited with a New Guinea comrade simply walking down the street in the United States. Paul spent almost a year in Guam and one year in the Philippines.

"It is bad when you have to face your enemy. The Air Force is over you, heavy equipment is behind you, and the enemy is in front of you." Paul Masalko was a foot soldier. He walked all the way up the east coast of New Guinea, was wounded, and received a Purple Heart. "People will never know unless they are a part of it [war] how miserable it is." He continued, "How long does it take to forget what you've seen?" War plagued Paul's thoughts for sixty-four years. He described some downtime in the jungle where the soldiers played poker. He did not have any money and borrowed ten dollars from another soldier. Two days later, the soldier got killed. "I still owe him ten dollars. For sixty-four years, I've owed him ten dollars."

In the Philippines, Manila was demolished, and "it stunk so bad. Dead people were buried. Nothing stinks like a rotten person." Paul described dead Japanese corpses covered in flies. He spotted a biscuit covered with flies. Hunger drove him to wipe away the flies and eat the biscuit. They ended up putting diesel fuel on the dead enemy bodies to get the flies off of them. He stated again, "No one will ever unknow unless you are part of it [war]."

Paul shared that he spent almost fifty months to the day of his young life at war. "I am a survivor," he states. He showed me his draft card—drafted October 20, 1941, discharged December 17, 1945.

Times were not always so bad as a soldier. When he was stationed at Fort Leonard, Missouri, he never had to wait very long for a ride home from strangers. There were plenty of good Samaritans at that time that brought soldiers home for the weekend, took them places, and made them feel at home. Once when Paul was stationed in California, he only had enough money for fare home and fifty cents leftover. He still had fifty cents when he arrived home due to the generosity of others.

He drifted back to war memories stating, "It was hell. No one will ever know."

I asked him what he would like future generations to know about war. He seemed concerned that some younger people don't pay any attention to history. Then he said, "War is frightening." He described being in the jungle again and being set up for an ambush. He and other soldiers were taken by a boat ten miles up the coast and dropped off in enemy territory where they killed the enemy, trying to survive the three-day-and-three-night mission. When the time came to be relieved, the new team was one-man short, requiring Paul to endure another three days and three nights in enemy territory. Paul ended up briefing the new commander who was relieving his original group. They walked down a cow path area to a big field when all of a sudden, he was face-to-face with the enemy. Paul froze. He looked death in the face. He did not want to die. He didn't finish the story. Instead, he described all the bullet holes in his clothes and how he lost war memorabilia in transit home. He obviously survived his war injuries.

As the number one scout in New Guinea traveling down another cow path, he wondered, *How much time have I got?* Suddenly without warning, a cockatoo bird took off over his head, creating intense fear and trepidation. He described the goose pimples that covered his body. Paul said, "I am not a hero. I'm not superman. There's enough [during war] to upset a man with a cast iron stomach."

In reviewing an extract from the *Cockatoo* news summary, Sixth Infantry Division, the Philippines, dated Wednesday, March 28, 1945, the division notably set a record "for continuous combat against the Japanese on Luzon, and probably for the entire Southwest Pacific theater of operations, according to a press release passed by Gen Douglas MacArthur's headquarters Tuesday." The Sixth Infantry endured seventy-eight straight days of combat against the enemy and continued to assault the Shimbu Line east of Manila. The Sixth killed nine thousand Japanese and destroyed or captured enemy equipment such as tanks, armored cars, ammunition dumps, and caves of the enemy. The Sixth battled the enemy in Munoz and at the Shimbu Line in the Sierra Madre mountains east of Manila.

A Western Union telegram notified Private First Class Paul Masalkos's family of him being wounded in action in Sanspor on August 25, 1944.

I spent time in Manila, Philippines in the late 1990s. While there, I visited the Manila American Cemetery. According to American Battle Monument Commission, abmc.gov, this cemetery sits on 152 acres and holds the largest number of graves of our military dead of World War II. Twenty-five mosaic maps reflect American forces that fought in the Pacific, China, India, and Burma. Exactly 16,859 graves from operations in New Guinea and the Philippines hold those lost in battle. Additionally, 36,286 names of the missing are honored on tablets; and I recognized a name from Ohio, Raymond Kostura, aviation machinist's mate second class, US Navy, missing January 8, 1945. He was buried at sea and earned a Purple Heart. Seeing that name at the time caught my attention and reached into my soul.

Paul Masalko showing me his Purple Heart

Paul Masalko showing me his Japanese flag

Akron Beacon Journal given to me by Paul Masalko

CHAPTER 10

MATTHEW VITARTAS (DECEMBER 13, 1921, TO DECEMBER 20, 2013)

Recorded December 21, 2005
LST 909, ship captain, Leyte bay

Matthew Joseph Vitartas attended the University of Pittsburg Industrial Engineering School prior to WWII. Following a visit by admirals to his school, he was encouraged to apply for a probationary commission for the military upon graduating from college in June. He attended Officer Indoctrination School at Fort Schuyler, New York. Matthew then trained at a naval gun factory in Washington, DC, for six weeks, and then he was assigned to Amphibious Forces LST training. A new LST 909 was being built, and eventually he received a crew of men and left Massachusetts on a journey through the Panama Canal, San Diego, Pearl Harbor, and landed in Leyte, Philippines.

Matthew proudly described landing on the beach in Leyte. He stood on the port side of the ship with two other men witnessing General McArthur's arrival. This thrilled Matthew and his shipmates. He showed me a photo of his ship which was 329 feet long.

The crew stayed in Leyte for a couple of weeks. As part of a flotilla, a fleet of about ten LSTs were ordered to leave Leyte. This duty requiring them to leave proved fortuitous. As they were leaving, Matthew and his men could hear off the port side of the ship; but they could not see the Battle of Samar, which was one of the largest naval battles in history which took place on October 25, 1944, and the Americans were not prepared. Matthew is certain that he and his men would have died had they still been present in that area. The Japanese had them on the run.

"Mindoro island in the Philippines was Japanese hell." The Battle of Mindoro took place from December 13–15, 1944. He was part of twelve to fourteen LSTs. Each LST pulled an army boat that carried a tank. He ran into an Army guy that was from the same town where he was born and raised. The LSTs had escorts which were cruisers, and there were four of them. Aircraft carriers were part of the group. At dusk, a kamikaze came in and hit a cruiser resulting in a fire. A P38 plane suddenly came out of the clouds, flipped, and went after a Japanese kamikaze. Japanese surrounded them, and they had to move quickly when landing the smaller boats on the beaches delivering personnel, materials, and supplies.

Nine to eleven kamikazes sought to destroy Matthew's LST and crew. He and another man witnessed a kamikaze coming straight for them just thirty feet away. By the grace of God, the kamikaze dove into the water and did not hit its target, LST 909.

Lingayen Gulf amphibious allied invasion took place January 6–9, 1945. Matthew landed on the beach head on D-Day plus two. They traveled from island to island.

"Okinawa had a lot going on," he shared with me. He held the duty of caring for his troops, and kamikazes threatened their survival. He described typhoons as they ripped through the area. He recalls watching the USS *Pittsburg* from afar as 100 feet of bow ripped off, as 138-foot waves sent the ship air-bound only to slam down on the water. The ship survived, and she made port. One man lost his life. Twenty-one ships survived the typhoon. Matthew was not frightened and said, "There was nothing you could do about it." He went about his regular duties.

Matthew visited Hiroshima and Wake Island during WWII. The United Stated detonated two bombs over Hiroshima and Nagasaki on August 6 and 9, 1945, resulting in allied victory when Japan surrendered to the Allies on August 15, 1945. Wake Island that had a harbor serving the same purpose as Pearl Harbor housing ships was attacked simultaneously with Pearl Harbor (attacked on December 7, 1941). Approximately 449 Marines of the First Dense Battalion and VMF-211 were on the island at the time of the attack, resulting in 49 killed and 32 wounded in action. The rest became prisoners of war. Sixty-eight Navy personnel occupied the island at that time, and three were killed and five were wounded. The army did not lose any soldiers. Seventy civilians were killed, and twenty wounded. The Battle of Wake Island lasted from December 8, 1941, to December 23, 1941. Japan won the battle and held onto the island until Japan surrendered it on September 4, 1945.

Matthew Vitartas became commanding officer in Guam and ended his military career in San Francisco. He states he did his duty and chokes up about the flag and the "Star-Spangled Banner" to this day. Matthew felt he never proved himself. He was close to action, could hear the action, but not see it. He and his crew simply got material and people to the beachheads. He described a conversation with his son, Paul, and stated, "How can you be a coward on a ship? I had no direct contact [with the enemy]."

Matthew mentioned Russia invading Japan just before the Japanese surrendered. He and two of his comrades felt ready to go after Russia because Russia was the real enemy; but they believed politics got in the way.

Matthew Vitartas showing me his ship

CHAPTER 11

RICHARD H. STAMBAUGH

I received a letter dated October 5, 2009, from Bruce Stambaugh, son of Richard H. Stambaugh,

> Dear Dr. Drumm, thank you so much for ensuring that our father, Richard H Stambaugh, was able to participate in the September 12, 2009 Honor Flight from Akron-Canton Regional Airport. I am so thankful that you "pulled some strings" for Dad. I was especially moved when I saw you at the airport welcoming Dad home. That was above and beyond the call of duty. But having had the honor to meet you several times during Dad's appointments with you, I wasn't surprised that you would do such a compassionate, loving act.
>
> Dad and I recently gave a slideshow presentation about the Honor Flight at Walnut Hills Retirement Home in Walnut Creek, where MIT comes right after my marriage. That is testimony enough to show just how much this opportunity meant to Dad. My brother, Craig, and I were honored to be able to accompany Dad on the trip.

Bruce wrote,

> Dr. Drumm, you have ben an absolute blessing to not only our father, but to the entire family. We thank you for your wonderful, kind treatment and love you have shown not only Dad, but to us all. I have enclosed a story I wrote about the Honor Flight with Dad, and a copy of the column I write for our local weekly newspaper. Again, thanks so much, and may God continue to richly bless you. Bruce Stambaugh

I give God all the glory and I praise His holy name. Jesus commands us to love one another like He loved us. I give God the glory that sometimes I was able to show love toward others. This is my main goal in life. I believe Jesus meant it when He said to love others as ourselves.

Bruce granted me permission to share his story.

In honor of the day, my late father, and the visionary
founders who penned our freedoms

My father, Richard H. Stambaugh, achieved a long-time goal when he was able to visit the World War II Memorial in Washington, DC, on September 12, 2009, thanks to Honor Flight. As part of a photographic review of the twenty-first century's first decade, this picture appeared on the front page of the NewYorkTimes.com on December 24, 2009, three days after Dad died.

The original article was first published on November 11, 2011. I am republishing a revised version today in honor of Veterans Day in the US and for all those who work globally for peace.

The very first sermon I heard preached in a Mennonite church 40 years ago was on nonresistance. That was precisely what I was looking for spiritually, and I embraced it. My father, a World War II veteran, was skeptical, but eventually accepted my decision.

Now years later, I was to accompany my 89-year-old father on a special excursion called Honor Flight for World War II vets. Dad was dying of cancer, and he had long wanted to make this trip to Washington, D.C. Regardless of physical condition, each of the 117 vets on the plane was required to have a guardian for the all-day round-trip. Given his physical situation, Dad needed extra care.

Given my nonresistance stance on war, I was reluctant to go. I likely would be the only conscientious objector on the packed plane. But this trip wasn't about me. It was about my father fulfilling one of his dreams. To help him accomplish that, regardless of my personal convictions, I needed to go with him.

My older brother, Craig, and I with our father, Dick, prior to leaving Akron-Canton Airport. Craig served as guardian for two other vets on the day-long trip.

As anticipated, the vets received their patriotic just due. Upon arriving at Reagan National Airport in Washington, DC, fire trucks sprayed arches of water across our arriving jetliner. This ritual was usually reserved for dignitaries. As we exited the plane and entered the terminal, a concert band played patriotic music. Red, white, and blue balloons were everywhere; and hundreds of volunteers vigorously greeted us.

Another veteran was the first to welcome Dad to the
World War II Memorial in Washington, DC.

At the circular, mostly granite World War II Memorial, strangers came up to the vets and shook their hands and thanked them for their service. I emotionally took it all in, focusing my attention on caring for my elderly father.

The entourage visited several other war monuments in the U.S. capital that day, too. Back at the airport, we had left in the morning, the vets received a similar patriotic welcome home. Dad said this experience ranked right behind his 67-year marriage.

With that comment, I was exceedingly glad that I had had the chance to experience that day with my father. I felt honored to have been able to accompany him on his most significant day and glad he had gotten to go. Dad died three months later.

Despite all the hoopla of that day or perhaps because of it, the futility of war became all the more obvious to me and had actually reinforced my nonresistance stance. To a person, the vets with whom I spoke said they hated what they had had to do.

Hundreds of well-wishers greeted the vets upon their return to Ohio.

For a day I had had one foot on the foundation of God and country, and the other on the teachings of Jesus. I also remembered the words of Jesus, when he said to turn the other cheek and go the second mile and beyond for your enemy. The trip with my father was an inspirational reminder of the commitment I had made as a young man to a different way of making peace in a hostile world.

Each vet on the Honor Flight received letters to read during mail call on the flight home.

Because of this experience, I had bonded with my father in his time of need, and I greatly respected what my father and the other veterans on the flight had done. And yet, I knew I could not have done what they had, not because of cowardice, but out of conviction.

I had participated in the Honor Flight out of love and respect for my earthly father. I had held fast to my peace convictions out of love and devotion to my father in heaven. In that paradox,

I had found no conflict whatsoever. (Written by Bruce Stambaugh, 2017)

When Dad spied Senator Bob Dole, who forged the way for the World War II Memorial, he rose out of his wheelchair and shuffled and squeezed his way beside the senator.

Dr. Lori Drumm taking a photograph of Charles Stambaugh as he arrived at CAK Airport

CHAPTER 12

HAROLD WALDROP

I met Harold Waldrop at Canton Community Outpatient Clinic when he established care with me as his primary care physician. At the time, I left out veteran tracts inviting veterans to know Jesus as their Lord and Savior. Harold invited me to church with him. New to the area and looking for a church, I accepted his invitation. We became friends. I enjoyed seeing Harold at church, and I believe he enjoyed seeing me there too. We came to meet one another's families over time.

Harold regularly participated in community events, and I attended community events regularly with my husband, Mark. It brought us joy to see Harold drive his WWII jeep with his friends in many parades. Eventually, Harold invited me to ride with him and other veterans in a parade which thrilled and honored me. To get to know the other veterans filled me with joy that is indescribable. To me, they were all heroes. What did I do to deserve being embraced by such an elite crowd? They welcomed me with open arms and treated me like a comrade. They were proud yet humble simultaneously. They gave their time regularly, participating in numerous community events that thrilled audiences of all ages. I smiled with delight every time I spotted them in a parade, and I really beamed when I rode in Harold's jeep on Memorial Day.

I cared for Harold at the Canton VA during my eight years at that location. When I relocated to VA Central Iowa Health Care

System in Des Moines, Iowa, we kept in contact by way of his wife. Martha and I wrote letters and sent cards. Martha had beautiful penmanship and stated Harold asked her to write. I received a letter dated, December 23, 2010. She thanked me for the Christmas card and for sending them our new address. Harold stopped going to the VA for care and had many local competent specialists. Martha filled me in on Harold's health. They were reading the Bible from beginning to the end out loud to each other and enjoying their reading time. Harold missed going to church but listened to the services every Sunday morning. She requested some pictures sometime, and I wonder if I ever sent them any. I hope I did.

I received another letter from Martha and Harold dated February 20, 2011. She wrote, "Needless to tell you that your letter was the very brightest spot in Harold's day!" Oh, thank you Lord that I wrote to them! They filled us in on Canton Baptist Temple pastors' activities and thanked us for contributing to military week camp. Camp CHOF is an amazing camp for children. We loved bringing our horses out there, and Mark and his horse, Bailey, were in a play once at the camp. They told us about an outing they had to Hometown Buffet with their daughter, Carole, and her husband, Richard, along with their daughter, Melinda, and family. Since they only went out for doctors' appointments, this sounded like a big deal to Harold and Martha. She asked who we rooted for during the Super Bowl game, and again I wondered if I ever answered her question. Her letters blessed us.

I found another card that was not dated, but she wished me well in my new position at the VA. I smiled as I read, "Harold appreciates that you keep in touch—he's very fond of both of you and I thank you for doing it."

Harold Waldrop and his WWII buddies

North Canton parade

The North Canton parade participants

Faircrest Middle School Veterans Day event

Memorial Day Canton parade: Ted Adamski, Lori
Drumm, Harold Waldrop in Harold's WWII jeep

Memorial Day, May 29, 2006, Robert Derga, father of
Cpl Dustin Derga, USMC, and Lori Drumm

Each flag honored military service members who gave their lives
for our country, the ultimate sacrifice.

CHAPTER 13

VICTOR FOX

Victor Fox served in the Korean War. Victor joined the Marine Corps after quitting Canal Fulton High School in 1948 when he was a junior. I served Victor as his primary care physician at Canton Community Outpatient Clinic. Victor spoiled us at the clinic, often bringing treats for the staff and other tokens of appreciation. I remember one extremely generous gift he gave to Mark and me after we came back from Hurricane Katrina. At the time, the gesture embarrassed me because the attention on us seemed not to be warranted. We went to Pass Christian, Mississippi, to give back to the community wrecked by the hurricane. Victor so wanted to join us; but we did not know what we would encounter on our journey. Instead of being angry, he had a plaque made to honor our efforts. It broke my heart. In retrospect, his generosity was God-given. He could not give enough of himself to others in need, including others without need! I now cherish the plaque he gave us, and it now reminds me of a man of God who showed God's love to everyone around him.

Victor and Sandy Fox, Mitch Leibsla, at Canton Baptist Temple

August 4, 2006, Hall of Fame visitor who came to Canton
Community Outpatient Clinic with Victor Fox, veteran

CHAPTER 14

ROYAL WEISEL

I met Royal Weisel at Canton Community Outpatient Clinic when he established care with me as his primary care physician. He and his wife, Janet, became good friends. They faithfully attended community events, especially veteran-related events held on Memorial Day and Veterans Day. They surprised me at Canton Akron Airport during an Honor Flight CAK event. I loved running into them, and I soon anticipated their presence when I attended gatherings.

I believe I served Royal Weisel as his primary care physician for about eight years. I transferred to VA Central Iowa Health Care System in 2010; but we kept in touch over the years. Royal and Janet appreciated the care they received from the VA, often mentioning their gratitude in the cards they sent. After relocating to Iowa, I received a special Christmas card from Janet and Royal. They wrote,

> You can't imagine how missed one super doctor can be! The nurse taking blood for coumadin just tears up when your name is mentioned… You have given me so much strength—I will handle my part. A reason for everything. You and Mark and "Mr. Bagpipes" are precious to us. Be blessed. So glad our paths crossed!

Royal Weisel passed away on January 20, 2013, at the age of eighty-three years. He was a Korean War veteran and recipient of two bronze stars. He worked for Essroc and was a retired farmer. His obituary states, "The proudest moment for Royal was to be chosen for the Honor Flight to Washington, DC." He enjoyed ballroom dancing. He was loved and cherished by his family. I received a heartfelt letter from Janet informing me of Royal's death. She wrote,

> You did so much for Royal and we sure miss having you nearby-you have so much more to do for veterans. We feel so blessed and honored to have received such care and the Honor Flight was so important to us—Our gratitude to you… Thanks for helping him to be part of my life for so many more years.

In another card arriving in May the same year, Janet wrote,

> Dearest Dr. Lori and Mark, Next weekend we celebrated Memorial Day, a day to pay tribute and give thanks to all who served and have served the wonderful country and one another. I pray and thank God for both of you. Royal's ashes were placed beside his parents for Mother's Day and both our plaques have been put in place for Memorial Day—what an honor! Continue to make this world a better place and know your efforts are so greatly appreciated. Thank you… Love you both, Jan Weisel.

In a letter from Janet (Jan) dated August 29, 2015, she mentioned the passing of James Stevens at the age of ninety-one years. She wrote, "You had so many patients that adored you. How wonderful." Jan and I became penpals. We still write good old-fashion letters to each other and send them by snail mail. We cherish hand-written letters and we both look forward to the next letter.

In one letter Jan wrote, "So excited to receive your update—you do live an extremely colorful life… I did attend the Veterans Day memorial, and you were with me in spirit." She mentioned Royal's youngest son stops by to check on her, and she wrote, "He looks and smiles just like Royal." Jan closed with "Pray for you and feel so blessed to touch base—You are the sunshine in my life and inspiration to face each day—I am so grateful!!" Jan continued to attend Veterans Day and Memorial Day community events no matter what the weather brought. One year she wrote, "This year again on Nov 11, the same group assembled. We all froze to death but we did it with a smile-wouldn't miss it for the world."

I don't think Jan ever missed sending me a Veterans Day card all of these years, and she sent me cards just because. She is a hoot too writing about all of the chores she does daily, including the line, "Friday is fun day—will have an affair with my weed whip. I have such a limited fun circle!"

Memorial Day parade, Canton, Ohio, 2006;
Lori Drumm, Royal, and Janet Weisel

Janet Weisel, Mr. Bagpiper Maxwell Leibsla, Royal Weisel

Royal Weisel, Honor Flight

CHAPTER 15

JAMES H. MCCORMICK AND REV. DR. DONALD W. FAIRCHILD

I served James McCormick as his physician at the VA. His wife, Martha, always came prepared for her husband's medical appointments with all of his medications and questions she had for me related to the health of James. I admired Martha from the beginning. We became very good friends, especially after James left this earth to join his Savior in heaven, Jesus Christ. After Martha suffered a major illness, she lived in a nursing home in Newcomerstown, Ohio. Mark, the boys, and I would visit Martha as regularly as we could. We moved to Iowa in 2010, and Martha always asked me, "How is I-O-Way?" I can still hear her sweet voice asking me about Iowa, pronouncing it i-o-way. Whenever we went back to Cleveland to see family, Mark and I made a point of visiting Martha. We loved surprising her. She would then immediately call her sons, Ronnie and Earl, to come to the nursing home to see us. Mark and I had the honor of meeting other McCormick family members visiting Martha. James and Martha's children and spouses are J. Earl and Sandy McCormick and H. Ronald and Janice McCormick of Newcomerstown and Sandy and Dr. Franklin Giampa of East Lansing, Michigan. They also have one granddaughter. I am sure Martha is happy in heaven with Jesus and her beloved husband, James. They were married for over sixty-five years.

July 9, 2005, sixty-fifth wedding anniversary at St. Paul Lutheran Church. James H. McCormick (eighty-eight years) and Martha L. McCormick (eighty-three years). "To my lovely Dr. and our friend."

Rev. Dr. Donald W. Fairchild
(March 14, 1923, to April 20, 2018)

Dr. Fairchild served in the Army as a PFC and earned lieutenant in the Navy. He served in World War II and Korea according to his obituary. I knew him as a veteran, dentist, and artist when I served him as his physician. He dropped off photographs of his paintings to share with me when I worked at the Canton VA. I cherish these photographs.

Donald graduated from the Ohio State University with a degree of doctor of dental surgery and practiced dentistry in Cambridge, Ohio, for forty-four years until his retirement in 1989. God called him into the ministry in 1967, and he served as a pastor until his retirement from ministry in 2006. I am certain Jesus greeted Rev. Dr. Donald W. Fairchild with the words, "Well done, my good and faithful servant."

Photograph courtesy of Rev. Dr. Donald Fairchild

CHAPTER 16

DON MILLIKEN, HONOR FLIGHT CAK AND VETERAN

Don Milliken sent me his testimony and a poem he wrote:

$7.50 a day! That's what Uncle Sam pays to soldiers, sailors, airman and marines in addition to their regular pay to go war aka combat pay is $7.50 a day. I've recently read a lot of posts stating that front line workers fighting the current pandemic should get hazard pay and those of us in education should get significant stipends if we have to teach in person during the pandemic.

During my twenty-eight years of service, I had eleven combat deployments in three declared wars and numerous other deployments that were in "hazardous areas" but weren't combat. During that time, I flew almost 500 combat sorties. There may have been a day or two where I actually earned my $7.50. One of those occasions happened in 2004 flying in to Balad, Iraq just a couple days before my 20th wedding anniversary.

We were coming down short final with damage in the #1 engine. The copilot declared an emergency with tower. I radioed command post the we were making an emergency landing and they needed to roll the fire trucks. During this process they asked "how many souls on board." I responded thirty-eight on board but I am pretty sure three are soulless. The pilot and engineer were shutting down #1 when it burst into flames. Tower immediately notified us that our left wing appeared to be on fire. The CO told them we know and we are handling it. Command post radios that the fire depart says the left wing is on fire. I replied "we know and we are looking for marsh mellow sticks." We land, the engineer gets the fuel flow shut off and the fire bottle discharged and the fire is put out. After our pax (passengers) are safely off of aircraft and the fire dept allows us, we go back in to collect our things. I radio command post to tell them we will be spending a few days until they can get a combat repair team flown in to change our engine and repair the wing damage. They call back that we need a MOFO/MEFE count for billeting. I had been in twenty years and thought I knew all of the acronyms but that one was new to me (male officers/female officers, male enlisted/female enlisted) so I gave them the only reply that came to mind. "We have six bad MOFO's on this airplane."

Later that night at the chow hall we were local celebrities. We had landed at dusk and a lot of bored airman and soldiers were treated to the light show when we flew down finally. Those

with radios kept asking who was the guy making
smart remarks while you were working the emergency? They couldn't believe someone would do
that. What they didn't know was I had earned my
$7.50 another day five years earlier during the
Kosovo war when I had faced a similar situation.

That day we took off out of Germany headed
toward Kosovo with a planeload of MRE's (mis-
siles, rockets and explosives). We determined that
the army pallets weights were not correct because
we were overloaded and flying like a stuck pig
barely able to climb. Then #2 engine overheated
and we had to shut it down. Now we are losing
altitude and determine we have to jettison fuel.
The copilot informs the French controllers we
are about to dump fuel. They immediately state
request denied. He tells them it is not a request
because we either dump fuel or pallets of high
explosives or we turn into a smoking hole in the
Ardennes. They got the point. To compound
matters we were surrounded by thunderstorms
and my radar decides to go tango uniform so
now we are flying blind in the weather. In the
middle of the fuel dump, we see lightening off
of the nose. In unison the crew yells stop dump.
Seconds later we are struck by lightning and it
fry's our avionics and most electrical relays. Now
we are limping in with only gravity feed in the
fuel tanks and very few instruments. As we are
rolling down the runway, the fire department
relays that we are leaking like a sieve. When we
pull off of the runway and abandon the aircraft,
we look at all of the charring and multiple exit
holes and wondered how we were standing there.
Later that night at the club guys kept asking me if

I was the one on command post and were telling me they could hear the tension in my voice. After the third time of hearing this I determined that never again would anyone know I was anything but cool during an emergency. From that day on I would take a few breaths and put on my best radio voice and make a few jokes anytime I was in an aircraft with an emergency.

Back to 2004 Balad, when we made our way to the air force area of the camp that night, there was no power because their generator farm had been hit by a mortar earlier that day. The airman told us we would have to look through the tents using flashlights to find empty cots. I found a cot in tent full of young security forces airman. The billeting guy also told us we should lie down on the floor until the all clear if we heard the warning sirens. I was just about to go to sleep when I heard a couple of explosions and the first siren went off. I noticed not one of the airmen left his cot to lie down on the filthy floor. So, I decided to get back into my cot. A couple hours later I had finally fallen asleep when there were more booms and another siren. I laid there thinking I sure earned my $7.50 today!

Ladies and gentlemen, life is a risk. There is never zero risk in anything. The air force has spent years learning how to deal with risk and how to mitigate risk when they can. But the missions have to be flown. We just had to figure out how to do it as safely as possible and still accomplish the mission. Sometimes we had to accept more risk than at other times. When it all goes to hell, we need to put on our bravest faces and our best radio voices and deal with the adversity.

Our children and their future are at risk
now if we ignore the American Academy of
Pediatrics advice and continue to lock them
away. 167,000 pediatricians say we are doing
more damage locking them away than the virus
is doing to this very low risk population. Look at
the statistics and the scientific evidence. Look at
the European's they are educating their children
in person. Students need to be in school. Those
of us who are entrusted to educate them need to
figure out how we can do this safely.

Yes, we educators and staff are at risk—we
need to mitigate it. I am approaching sixty and I
am a cancer survivor with internal damage left by
multiple surgeries, but I still want to go back into
the classroom. That said, I will figure out how to
keep myself safe.

If we can send our young men and women
to war for $7.50 a day, we need to figure out how
to deal with risk without asking for thousands in
compensation that our districts don't have. My
next post will deal with all of the risk mitigation
strategies I learned while flying in the air force.

I was commissioned into the Air Force in June of '84 and retired from the Air Force nine years ago this week in June of 2012. In those twenty-eight years I got to travel and see things that this small-town kid could have never imagined. I have been all over South America, Africa, Europe, the Middle East and parts of Asia. I have met Senators, Congressmen, Foreign Generals, Ambassadors and a Prime Minister. I had eleven combat deployments adding up to over 450 combat sorties and 1000+ hours of combat time.

I have worn the uniform since I was a freshman ROTC cadet at Ohio State in 1980. I have the privilege of continuing to wear it as a retiree teaching JROTC. I get notes and messages all of the time from former students and players letting me know I continue to make an impact and I am grateful for that opportunity. However, I am not going to lie, I do miss flying and the guys and gals I flew with.

I wrote these words below as part of my retirement speech in 2012. I know some of you have seen it before but I would like to rededicate it on the anniversary of my retirement. I dedicate it to those who have gone before and those who are still serving. (Written by Don Milliken)

*****

I Am an American Serviceman

I am an American Serviceman.
Some in this world say I walk with arrogance.
Some of my own countrymen call me a cowboy.
They have not been where I have been.
They have not seen the places where tyrants take freedom with the barrel of a gun.
Places where evil men take life with impunity.

I go to these places wearing my country's flag.
In the name of this country, I deliver food, clothing, shelter, and security.
But most of all, I bring hope and freedom.
I also carry out the bodies of my countrymen who gave their all—battling tyrants in the name of justice and freedom.

My country and my comrades ask only that those who benefit from our presence, cherish what we have sacrificed to bring them.

No, it is not arrogance in my step.
It is the firm resolve of one, who has been to and returned from, the dark places of this world.
One who walks side by side with his comrades in arms, knowing that together they have the strength
to prevail when challenging the darkness.
One who must show confidence and not fear when confronting this evil.

I have answered the call.
I share the bond with others, who say,
"Who if not me?"
I am an American Serviceman.

CHAPTER 17

CANTON FOOTBALL HALL OF FAME VISITS AND PARADES

Hall of Fame Visit August 4, 2006

Each year, Football Hall of Fame recipients would come to the Canton VA to visit the veterans. As employees of the VA, we joined in the fun.

Maria Lahmers sports two Super Bowl rings.

Year 2008 Canton Football Hall of Fame parade

Shirley Toland invited me to participate in many Canton Hall of Fame parades on the Canton VA float. What an honor! I met the most amazing heroes at these parades. We rode together on an amazingly well-attended parade route for miles, waving to the crowds who cheered us on and shouted, "Thank you for your service!" My face hurt by the end of the parade from smiling so much. Riding in parades as a veteran, along with other veterans, heroes in my opinion, blessed my soul.

WWII POW, PFC Robert W. Ludwig Sr., Army; WWII POW Louis S. Turansky, Air Force; WWII POW Staff Sergeant Herman White, Air Force, in the 2008 Canton Football Hall of Fame Parade. Photo by Shirley Toland.

Herman White served in WWII from 1942 to 1944. He flew on a B25 airplane for the Air Force. His plane was shot down in Italy on his forty-fourth mission. The plane landed in the mountains of Italy. He was captured and turned over to the Germans. He married after the war, and they had a son, Herman.

WWII POW, PFC Floyd Kohr, Army, my patient; WWII POW, PFC Louis Codian, Army; Korean POW, Sergeant George VanPelt, Army, in the 2008 Canton Football Hall of Fame Parade. Photo by Shirley Toland. Not pictured: POW Karl Shank due to illness.

Back row: Chuck Siefer, Michael Lee, Lori Drumm, Robert Ludwig, George VanPelt Front row: Robert Hahn, Don Miller, Floyd Kohr, Louis Codian, Louis Turansky

Don Miller served in WWII and Korea. He earned a Bronze Star and Purple Heart. Robert Hahn served in WWII as a merchant marine in the European Theater. He accompanied me in the Canton Hall of Fame Parade, rode with me on Honor Flight CAK, and attended Veterans Day festivities at Faircrest Memorial Middle School.

Canton Football Hall of Fame Parade 2009, 2010. Maxwell Leibsla, bagpiper, stepson. Photo courtesy of Shirley Toland.

Photographs courtesy of Shirley Toland

I have both of my hands in the air waving to the crowd.

CHAPTER 18

CANTON VA PATIENTS

Jessica Clements

It was an honor to meet and care for Army Staff Sergeant Jessica Clements at the Canton VA. Her story blew me away. The braveness of Jessica along the long road to healing astounded me. The care she received by our military medics, surgeons, nurses, physical therapists, occupational therapists, mental health providers, and other support staff resulted in saving Jessica's life. My mind cannot imagine everything that transpired for me to have the privilege to provide this war hero primary care.

The Repository newspaper reporter, Fellicia Smith, interviewed Jessica at the YMCA's Senior Fun Club that hosted an event called "Tribute to Veterans" that Jessica and her grandfather, Harry Palmer, attended the event. Jessica was the guest speaker. Jessica shared her story about being "nearly killed in May 2004 by a roadside bomb in Iraq. Initially, she was given just a 2 percent chance to live. Four years later, Clements is a homeowner in Plain Township and a junior at the University of Akron." She was in a coma for six weeks and spent eleven months at Walter Reed Hospital. "Clements suffered a traumatic brain injury in Iraq. She had to relearn to walk, talk, read, write, and to bathe herself. She still has seizures related to the injury."

I looked forward to our visits at the clinic. She was delightful to care for, and I enjoyed hearing about her progress with her studies.

I often told Jessica's story to others to encourage them. I included her in presentations as an inspiration to me. Her comrades in Iraq are heroes too. They got Jessica to the right places at the right time. Every person Jessica encountered on her long road to recovery are heroes to me. I will never meet them; but I praise God for them and for God's healing hand on Jessica Clements's life. God obviously had big plans for her for the glory of His kingdom.

Akron Beacon Journal, Saturday, April 7, 2007, Jessica Clements holds a plastic model of her skull showing damage from a bomb explosion in Iraq.

GOOD FEELINGS Army Staff Sgt. Jessica Clements of Plain Township hugs her grandfather, Harry Palmer, at the Paul & Carol David YMCA on Wednesday. Clements was the featured speaker at a Tribute to Veterans program presented by the Senior Fun Club. Clements said positive words from her grandfather have helped her throughout her life.

Beating the odds

Former soldier who was seriously injured by roadside bomb in Iraq inspires crowd at veterans tribute

BY FELLICIA SMITH
REPOSITORY STAFF WRITER

JACKSON TWP.

The crowd was small, but the emotions inside an activity room at the Paul & Carol David YMCA on Wednesday were overwhelming. "I cried through the whole thing," Kay Demaskey of Jackson Township said as tears continued to well in her eyes. "I started when the music began. It touches me so."

The YMCA's Senior Fun Club hosted a Tribute to Veterans Wednesday afternoon at the recreational facility.

Army Staff Sgt. Jessica Clements, who was critically injured in Iraq, and Dr. Robert Wade, a World War II veteran,

spoke at the event. Veterans in the audience were asked to stand and be recognized as music from each branch of the service was played.

Clements, the featured speaker, was nearly killed in May 2004 by a roadside bomb in Iraq. Initially, she was given just a 2 percent chance to live. Four years later, Clements is a homeowner in Plain Township and a junior at the University of Akron.

Her story of survival — she spent 11 months at Walter Reed Hospital and was in a coma for six weeks — has been told on "60 Minutes," "The Oprah Winfrey Show" and other national news outlets.

"Be thankful for the little things you have," Clements implored attendees. She asked them not to

take anything for granted, whether it is their vision, legs or hearing.

"I don't take my legs for granted," said Clements, who didn't have the use of her legs as she recovered from her injuries.

"After I was injured, a side effect was I was put into a coma. I couldn't move my left side."

Clements suffered a traumatic brain injury in Iraq. She had to relearn to walk, talk, read, write and to bathe herself. She still has seizures related to the injury.

"I still have daily struggles," Clements said. "For the most part, I'm well."

Clements is working on a book about her challenges called "The Miracle Girl," and travels around

SEE ODDS

The Repository, Thursday, May 15, 2008, Army Staff Sgt. Jessica Clements with her grandfather, Harry Palmer

Elmer Zeni

Elmer Zeni, my patient from Canton VA, made this for me. It hangs in my office at Deer Lodge Medical Center in Montana.

Don Guildoo

When I learned that veteran Don Guildoo was Richard Marx's uncle, I flipped out with excitement. I became as silly as a schoolgirl when I shared with Don the big crush I had on Richard Marx in the 1980s and 1990s. I loved Richard's music, and he was so cute. He had a great thing going on in the big hair days as we all did.

I hung around my beautiful friend, Kim Eckhardt, at the time, and we made our way into the VIP section of Club Coconuts in the Cleveland Flats. We met many football players (such as Tim Manoa of the Cleveland Browns), baseball players (such as Mel Hall of the New York Yankees, Cleveland Indians), and music celebrities during our young years. One special outdoor concert took place in the Cleveland flats, and Richard Marx did not disappoint us. We had great seats, and the night ended magically.

Later in life, Mark and I learned of a free outdoor concert during the Jackson Community Celebration at North Park in Canton, Ohio, featuring Richard Marx in July of 2004. I wiggled my way up to the front telling everyone I had to get up close because I honestly love Richard Marx. Mark did not seem to mind. People laughed at me and let me move up closer to the stage. All of us in the audience sang along with Richard that evening. We all loved Richard Marx, and we all knew the words to his songs.

Don Guildoo got a kick out me gushing over his nephew and brought me a personally autographed photograph of Richard. I still have it, of course. He also tried to arrange a backstage meeting with his nephew when we traveled to see Richard in Toledo. The meeting did not occur; but I enjoyed every minute of being in the audience. I bought a t-shirt that night too.

I met Gary Guildoo also, Don's brother. I don't remember if I was his primary care provider or if the nurses just came to me all excited and brought me to say hi to Gary. I used to joke with my nurses that I hoped Richard Marx would not surprise me by stopping by the clinic because I knew I would faint. It would have been just too much for me to handle. That's how much of a crush I had on him in my thirties. The nurses would rush to tell me when one of Richard's uncles came to the clinic; and I, of course, dropped everything to catch up on the latest and greatest Richard Marx news.

To my great fortune, I recently reconnected with Don. I sent him a card requesting his permission to include him along with Richard in my book. He surprised me with a telephone call as Mark and I headed back to Ohio for Thanksgiving. Don is eighty-three years old now; and his brother, Gary, is doing amazingly well at the age of eighty-seven. Don speaks with Richard regularly and received Richard's book about his memoirs. I ordered the book right after speaking with Don, of course. I cannot wait to read it!

Don spends his days drawing, mostly birds. He's drawn many pictures, and it sounds like he has quite the talent. He helps his granddaughter draw also, and she is quite talented he shared. I picture him grinning ear to ear as he speaks of her.

Don Guildoo served in the US Air Force as an aircraft mechanic. He enjoyed his scenic duty station in Hawaii. He raised two girls and a boy. Presently, he resides in Salineville, Ohio, with his wife.

I still get goose bumps just remembering my young years and the thrills that came with my music crushes. Kim and I almost met Rick Astley once at Club Coconuts. We had people tell us he wanted to meet us; but it did not happen. We did hang out with Kevin Raleigh regularly from the Michael Stanley Band when he came out with his solo album, *Delusions of Grandeur*. I drove him and others crazy talking about Jesus and salvation at Club Coconuts. I became known as the psychologist of the club.

RICHARD MARX

Autographed photograph of my heartthrob, Richard Marx. Don Guildoo, his uncle, sent this to me and wrote, "Hi Lori, hope this makes your day! Maybe I'll see you at the Toledo concert. Best of luck, Don." I received the photograph on or about September 2, 2009.

Paul Mossor

I found an undated letter from Craig Mossor, veteran Paul Mossor's son. He wrote,

> Hi Lori, I just wanted to thank you for writing my Dad-it made his Christmas to hear from you! He lives with us now so that is why your last letter was returned although I am not sure why they did not forward it-mabe it was before I did the change of address... Anyway, I wanted you to know how grateful I am that you care so much about my Dad—it means soooo much to him. I do not know if you know it or not, but you are an Angel on Earth! I hope all is well with you and your new job—it sounds like you are doing fine. If you ever have a desire or need to visit Canton, let us know and I will pay your airfare. God Bless, Craig Mossor.

Paul Mossor wrote,

> Dear Dr. Drumm. Thank you for the Christmas card. You can't ever know in this lifetime how much it meant to hear from you. You are in my prayers twice a day and you are still my main doctor. I felt I must write to you... I am glad that you and Mark are doing well. Horses were my hobby too. (Standard bred, Sulky) I used to race on the Grand Circuit.
> You look more beautiful every time that I see you. I keep looking to see you on the T.V, News about the election. Have a Happy New Year. I will look forward to hearing from you. Forever Yours, Paul Mossor.

As I write about Paul, some memories come to mind. He once told me that he had my photograph enlarged and hung it up on the wall like a celebrity photo. I laugh when I remember this, and I smile as I remember feeling pretty to some of my older patients. At that time, I was in my thirties, ran regularly, so I was slim although I never knew it at the time, and had long blond hair. I also remember Paul sharing that he never left his home other than to come and see me at the clinic. He shared it was the highlight of his day, week, month, and year.

I did not know anything about his love for horses. There was so much I never knew about the veterans I served. Our visits were once or twice a year for a twenty-minute medical appointment for the most part. Other visits took place at community events with brief interactions. I usually took their photograph which is why I can share them with you in *Serving Heroes*.

To be called an angel, thanked for writing, hugged during a visit, updated on medical ailments, and prayed for brings tears of joy and gratitude to my heart. These veterans and their families will never know how much they meant to me which is why I am writing this book. Most of my patients have passed from this earth at this time. I hope and pray I am honoring their legacies by documenting every veteran I can remember as I search through fifteen years of memory boxes that have moved from Ohio to Iowa, back to Ohio, and ultimately to Montana. I sought out permission to write and include the veterans' stories by contacting family, friends, organizations, and newspapers. May all of those who read this book remember men and women of the Greatest Generation and beyond and their supportive families.

Paul Mossor, Lori Drumm at East Sparta, Ohio

Mr. Bucksbarg

Postcard of the USS *Drum* SS228 given to me along with a pin from Mr. Bucksbarg on January 5, 2007. "The USS *Drum* was named for a large sea bass found off the North Atlantic and Gulf Coasts. Built at Portsmouth, New Hampshire, she was in 13 War Patrols, awarded 12 campaign stars and sank 15 Japanese ships totaling over 80,000 tons."

Russ Wood

I served Russ Wood as a primary care provider at the Canton VA. I ran into him unexpectedly when I spoke at the Malvern Memorial Day celebration in 2007. Russ made me a collage of the event which I have in my office at Deer Lodge Medical Center.

He wrote to me on May 25, 2011 after I moved to Iowa. He penned,

> Dear Dr. Drumm, what an unexpected plea-
> sure seeing you at the Canton Clinic... So glad
> to hear that you're doing well in your new posi-
> tion, you deserve the best! You are a fantastic doc-
> tor, a wonderful person, not to mention a lovely
> young lady. I consider myself very fortunate to
> have been your patient. Thank you for all that
> you've done for me. Since Memorial Day is fast
> approaching, my thoughts go back to 2007 and
> your address at Bethlehem Cemetery in Malvern,
> Ohio. I was looking through the photos of that
> day and saw this one, which I didn't include in
> your collage. I wanted you to have a copy—hope
> you will cherish this memory as I do. Your friend
> and former patient, Russ Wood.

I do cherish the photograph and the collage to this very day. Thank you, Russ Wood!

Lori Drumm and Russ Wood. Photograph from Russ Wood.

Marine PFC David Tope

I served PFC David Tope at the Canton VA in 2004. Only nine-teen years of age, he served as a Marine with the Second Battalion Second Marine Division in Iraq. A bomb blast injured him while on a mission one month prior to *The Repository* interview by Veronica Van Dress. Veronica wrote, "A convoy of soldiers as sent out to disarm a roadside bomb. It could have happened to any one of the 40 Marines on the assignment, but the explosion that followed injured only one-Tope."

The Repository, PFC David Tope and his fiancé, Katie Wallin

Leonard Zaleski (Cowboy Len)

I interviewed Leonard Zaleski at the Canton VA in August 2008. He and his brother, Al, sought after the western way of life. Leonard saw a trick roper and took a fascination to that. He bought a book on trick roping and taught himself how to perform. After mastering the skill, he booked public performances as an entertainer. Cowboy Len performed for over one hundred audiences in 1998. He performed publicly and privately through self-promotion, in addition to a booking agent. He received many accolades. "All talent comes from God," he told me during the interview.

Leonard taught trick roping to his son, Brian, when Brian was very young. Leonard wanted his son to walk in his footsteps. "I've had a great ride and I just thank God for every day. He's been good to me." He ended our interview with the parting words, "Adios and as Roy Rogers said, 'Happy Trails.'"

Cowboy Len, Leonard Zaleski

James Stevens

James Stevens, another patient of mine at the VA, became a special friend to me. He joined Mark and me on an Honor Flight CAK trip and attended Canton Baptist Temple with us as a guest on one occasion. Jimmy, young at heart, impressed us with his humor, friendship, huge smile, and playful mannerisms.

James "Jimmy" Stevens, age nineteen, Kuminy, China, after the war was over in Burma. Photo given to me by Jimmy.

Photograph given to me from Jimmy Stevens. He is in the center in a
suit coat with his wife next to him; he is surrounded by his family.

Other Veteran Patients

I received Christmas cards from Donald Storsin and his family,
Don and Barbara McCune who wrote "Semper Fi," Ted and Marge
Evans, Elmer Zeni, Olinda Murphy and Earl R. Eckles, Shirley and
Jimmie Gauze, John Rohrig, Russ Wood, Francis Aowad, Charles
Warfield, Jim Stevens who thanked me for getting him on the
Honor Flight that he will never forget, Bill Spatz also thanked me
for September 18 and the pictures and told me to keep up the good
work, and Anna Greegor who stated, "Will never forget you for all
your caring, kind, and loving care you give." These are simply a few
cards I found. I know I received many more over the years.

Jim Mapes from Jackson Township wrote to the newspaper
stating, "I would like to thank Dr. Drumm and nurse Linda at the
Canton VA clinic. I had a high fever and fast heart rate. I called the

VA; they said they would work me in. Dr. Drumm and nurse Linda spent five hours of their busy schedule making me well, and for this I truly thank both of them."

I came across a letter from Thomas Hadjian written to me on October 27, 2008.

> Dear Dr. Drumm: I want to thank you for the thorough, efficient, and professional examination you gave me last week. You also made me comfortable while completing the exam. You have the capacity to instill confidence to your patients. You also show empathy, not sympathy, to your patients, and your bedside manner is excellent. I feel fortunate to have you as my physician. Sincerely, Thomas H. Jadijian.

I received a letter from John Pyatt from Indiana in 2008:

> Dr. Lori Drumm and Staff, I just wanted to say "thank you" for the wonderful service I got from you guys. I was in Canton on business and had a stomach problem. Even though you guys had appointments all day and were very busy, you took time out of your day to see me. Your nurse took the time to walk me through everything and you showed me nothing but professional courtesy. You guys are *awesome* and I am glad to have gone to your VA. Thank you again for the *best* service I could have possibly gotten. Thanks again, John Pyatt from Indiana.

Working at the Canton VA, I did not have the time I needed to interview interested veterans for the Library of Congress due to my demanding schedule of patients. I used up most of my energy at work, and I had little energy left over by the end of the day. I would now like to mention some of the worthy veterans:

- Paul Kamerer: September 18, 1921, field medic S. Pacific
- Jack Richard Jones: WWII, Korean veteran
- Bernard Ott: WWII Army for three years, served in France, Germany, Austria for 230 days on the front line. He received two Purple Hearts.
- Douglas Bunn: He was the first POW of WWII, held longest in China. He fired the first shot of WWII and received the first Purple Heart. In researching Douglas Bunn, USMC veteran, he was captured by Japan and imprisoned at Shanghai War Prisoners Camp, Kiawgwan Shanghai 31-121, according to US National Archives.
- Gerald Edie died on August 25, 2009. He flew on Honor Flight CAK before he died with me. According to his obituary, he was a WWII Navy navigator aboard PBY water rescue planes. He and his wife, Thelma Newton, were married for sixty-eight years, and they had three children. After WWII, Gerald worked for over twenty years at Joy Manufacturing of New Philadelphia. I had the honor to meet his son, Rick Edie.
- Richard Robb was a truck driver in Bastogne, the European WWII theater.

CHAPTER 19

ALL IN THE FAMILY

Melvin Keith Drumm

My dad, Melvin Keith Drumm, was born on October 4, 1936; and he is still living in Ohio with his wife, Gay. My dad served his country in the United States Air Force from July 1955 to April 1959. He attended basic training at Lackland Air Force Base in San Antonio, Texas. He graduated from dental hygiene school, Great Lakes Training Command, and assigned to Oklahoma City Air Force Base as his permanent duty station. He joined a mobile dental unit for two and one-half years which consisted of two dentists, three airmen, one laboratory technician, two dental assistants, and a dental hygienist, my dad. They traveled from one radar squadron to another, serving about two hundred active-duty military and their families. Some of the small squadrons were located in Sweetwater, Duncanville, and Texarkana, Oklahoma. Airman First Class (A1C) Melvin Drumm spent his last year in Kalibak, Iceland, and was honorably discharged from the Air Force at McGuire Air Force Base in New Jersey. He headed home to Duluth, Minnesota, and attended the University of Minnesota, Duluth, for a quarter. He met my mother at the university. I was born in the near future; and my brother, Randy, appeared fifteen months after I entered the world.

My parents moved the family to the Minneapolis/Saint Paul area when my dad accepted a sales position at Robert Hall. I remember playing in the racks of clothing as a small child. He worked twelve hours a day, six days a week from 1960 to 1965. In 1965, my dad, Mel, saw an ad in the newspaper soliciting a dental salesman. He knew he had dental experience and sales experience, and he applied for the job. He worked for Lactona and sold toothbrushes and other dental items for ten years. Mel and his family relocated to Omaha, Nebraska. I remember Cryer Avenue and the neighborhood like it was yesterday. We moved again to the Minneapolis area after two years in Nebraska and lived in Fridley followed by Spring Lake Park for a total of three years. Then came news of another transfer, this time to Cherry Hill, New Jersey. We stayed four years on the East Coast until news came again that Mel received an offer from Cleve Dent, a dental company in the Cleveland, Ohio, area. We lived in North Olmsted, a west side suburb of Cleveland. My dad worked for the company for five years and ended up at the best company ever, Centrix, a dental company started by Dr. William "Bill" Dragan, a dentist and entrepreneur who started the company in 1970. Mel Drumm joined the company in 1980. A team of businessmen grew the company and created unique dental products, manufactured its products, and marketed the products to dentists. The company expanded its dental products over the years. After years of dedication and hard work, Mel Drumm became president of the company until he retired in April 2004.

After retirement in 2004, Mel and his wife enjoyed their home in Madison, Connecticut, until they joined other family members, relocating to Thornville, Ohio, where they enjoy boating on Buckeye Lake.

Melvin Drumm, US Air Force, with a recent reflection if you look closely

Welcome Home Melvin Drumm, Columbus Honor Flight

Mitchell D. Leibsla (My Stepson)

PFC Mitchell Leibsla joined the United States Army after graduation from high school. He graduated from basic training from Fort Knox, Kentucky, as part of First Platoon, E Company 2/81, "wardawgs" in March of 2004. He then headed for training as a tank driver at Fort Carson, Colorado. Mitch's ultimate duty station was in Iraq as a combat soldier. I understand from conversations with Mitch that tanks were not used much, if at all, in Iraq. Mitch became a sniper. He has not shared much beyond the title. We believe he keeps his war experiences inside of him, although his dad and grandma have heard some shockingly graphic descriptions intermittently of Mitch's memories about the war. He willingly served his country following the unexpected death of his brother, Matthew, just months before Mitch deployed for Iraq in 2005. Mark and I really put our faith in God during Mitch's deployment. The thought of losing another son so soon became a possibility. We leaned on Jesus and prayed daily for God's divine protection over Mitch and our military.

Mitch's tour of duty eventually ended, and he was honorably discharged from the US Army. We are proud of Mitch and his service to our country. Mitch has joined us in serving veterans on Honor Flight CAK trips to Washington, DC, and he visits us in Montana. He really seems to enjoy snowmobiling and four-wheeling in the mountains. We still continue to pray for Mitch and his brother, Maxwell, every day. We are proud of the boys and we love them dearly. We pray they seek and follow God's plan for their lives.

Fort Knox Graduation 2004. Matthew, Mark, Maxwell, Mitchell Leibsla

Leland Forrest

Leland "Grandpa Lee" Forrest, my stepgrandpa, served on the USS *Topeka* during World War II in the Pacific theater. I had the privilege to visit with him on many occasions over a time span of forty years. He lived to be over 105 years of age. We spent many holidays together when he lived in St. Clairsville, Ohio, with Alicia, my stepgrandmother. Later, we would visit at my dad and Gay's home on Buckeye Lake in Thornville, Ohio. Our last visits were to his assisted living accomodations which were quite impressive. I often gave him Navy-themed gifts, and he would light up with delight.

Young Leland Forrest

Jayna and Jim Browning, Steven and Silvia Gaston, Ian and Liam Browning, Gay Drumm, Ralph Hamilton, Mel Drumm, Grandpa Leland Forrest, and Ellen Hamilton

Jacob Drumm

My nephew, Jacob "Jake" Drumm, graduated from Great Lakes Training Center on February 6, 2020. Many of us watched Jake's graduation on television. Some of the family attended the graduation in person. Jake is currently stationed at Naval Station Pearl Harbor.

Amber Drumm Vaughn, Jacob Drumm, Castagna "Tawni" Drumm, my nieces and nephew. Photo courtesy of Gina Castagna. Jacob's graduation February 6, 2020.

James Momb (My Cousin)

My cousin, Jimmy Momb, retired from the United States Army.

James Momb

Lauren Johnson

I remember talking to my cousin Scott's daughter, Lauren Johnson, about the Navy Health Professions Scholarship Program at one point. Lauren proudly raised her right hand to serve our nation on May 25, 2019 as one of two people in the country to be chosen to be a Naval optometrist. Lauren graduated as an optometrist in May 2022. She will attend Officer Development School (ODS), a five-week training course for Navy staff corps officers. Following training, she received orders that she will be serving in Okinawa, Japan. Lauren is currently planning to make Navy service her career stating, "I plan to hopefully stay until they kick me out!"

Lauren states,

> I joined the Navy at my convenience because I wanted to do something that was out of my comfort zone and knew it would help me grow as a person along with being able to serve our country. By joining, I'll be helping sailors keep up standards in medical readiness so they are able to be the best at their job.

Lauren completed an externship rotation in San Diego with the Navy on "school orders" from August 2021 to December 2021. She worked in many clinics including Balboa Hospital Naval Station, North Island, Marine Corps Recruit Depot (MCRD), Miramar, Naval Training Center (NTC) Refractive Surgery Center. Lauren performed flight physicals, deployment exams, Marine recruit vision screenings, specialty contact lens fitting for corneal disease, emergency walk-in exams, and more. I am happy to say we both participated as part of the Navy's Health Profession Scholarship Program. I look forward to hearing more from Lauren as she serves our country.

Photo given to me from Lauren Johnson of her
Navy commission day, May 25, 2019

Norman Heppner

Norman Heppner served his country by joining the United States
Army in 1959 at Lakewood Armory in Ohio. He completed eight
weeks of basic training at Fort Knox in Kentucky followed by sixteen
weeks of artillery training at Fort Sill in Oklahoma. He started out as
private first class and earned the rank of sergeant first class prior to
his honorable discharge. As part of the Army National Guard, Norm
and his unit were called upon to protect Ohio citizens during the July
18–24, 1966 Hough riots in Cleveland, Ohio. His most memorable
moment was saving the life of a lieutenant who fell into a burn pit.

Norman Heppner

Nick Russin (Barbara Stasko Leibsla's "Uncle")

My sister-in-law, Barbara Leibsla, is a descendent of Nick Russin, a War World II veteran, who became part of a famous photograph taken by Louis Weinraub/NP Pool/AP Photo on June 7, 1944, during the Normandy invasion. Tim Lambert wrote an article titled "How a Pennsylvania Man Ended Up in an Iconic D-Day Invasion Photo."

Nick Russin, born on December 18, 1912, was from Lyndora, Pennsylvania. Private First Class Russin, landed on Omaha Beach by ship and then a Landing Vehicle Craft Personnel (LVCP) during Operation Overlord, the largest amphibious operation ever as described by Tim Lambert in his article dated June 5, 2019. Nick was saved three times during his time on the beach. As he and others exited the LVCPs, their one-hundred-pound packs, which were carried on their backs, made them sink in the deep water. The men floundered amidst carnage, debris, equipment, rafts, corpses, body parts all the while trying to evade flying bullets by enemy fire. Nick was initially pulled back into the LVCP by two comrades. He was then saved again by comrades upon his second attempt to end up on dry ground on Omaha Beach which was captured on film by Louis Weinraub.

Chester "Chet" Ewer

I must include Chester Ewer, Mr. Ewer to me, from my childhood as a member of the family. He served in the Korean War. His wife, Arlene, and four daughters, Lori, Linda, Lisa, and Leslie, became a significant part of my life as a young girl. I lived in Fridley, Minnesota. Our family moved into our home on the same street as the Ewers. The Ewer girls and I became friends. I spent much time at their house during my young years. I recall watching *Gilligan's Island* after school. Arlene Ewer became my Brownies (Girl Scouts) leader, and sometimes my mom assisted during meetings. The Ewer girls and I rode the bus to school, and I recall walking down to their house to ride the bus. We often played after school, and I spent many nights sleeping over at the Ewers. I still remember being afraid of their black cat that would claw me in the middle of the night. I chuckle.

I recall Mr. Ewer enjoyed hunting, particularly bear hunting. He enjoyed camping, and I would tag along with the family on camping trips. They always welcomed me.

We all have reconnected on Facebook. Mr. Ewer is still alive and doing well. Mrs. Ewer looks terrific too. I did not know that Mr. Ewer was a Korean veteran when I was a child. As an adult, I want to thank him for his service to our country so I could enjoy my childhood. My father, brother, husband, and I stopped by to see the Ewer family on at least two occasions when we visited Minnesota. It thrilled us to catch up with this wonderful family.

Chester Ewer. Photo courtesy of the Ewer family.

Leslie, Lisa, Arlene (Mrs. Ewer), Chet (Mr. Ewer), Lori,
Linda Ewer. Photo courtesy of the Ewer family.

CHAPTER 20

FINAL SALUTE

There are many more veterans I would like to mention and write about to honor all of those who influenced my life. I became a Navy doctor because of the influence of the Vietnam War I learned about as a child. Later, Vietnam veterans I served impacted my career as a physician while working for the Navy and then the VA for almost two decades.

Other veterans became like family, and I remember Pat and George Costatino from Groton, Connecticut. When I was on active duty, they would invite me over to their house for dinner, and we would then watch *60 Minutes* together on Sunday nights. George, an electrician, helped me with electrical work at my home and medical office in Westerly, Rhode Island. They were my first patients when I opened my private practice. We kept in touch for many years through cards and letters.

I worked with many veterans during my VA career. The person who stands out the most was my administrative officer at VA Northern Indiana Health Care System, Eric Self, Air Force veteran. He still actively serves veterans at the VA in Loma Linda, California. He proved to be an amazingly hard worker and loyal to our cause to serve veterans even when situations challenged us. I smile with admiration as I remember our service together in Indiana.

I remember Terry Odle who served with her husband, Kenny, Rocco and Cheri Palmer, and Howard Pooler from VA Northern

Indiana Health Care System, along with Dr. Miles "Lew" Sheffer from VA Central Iowa Health Care System.

Terry and Kenny Odle. Facebook photo by the Odles.

Rocco and Cheri Palmer. Facebook photo by the Palmers.

Howard Pooler

I participated in community events with many of my veteran coworkers on the Canton VA Hall of Fame Parade float for several years. We celebrated Veterans Day together which was commemorated in a collage one year.

Presently, I work with Dr. Scot Murray, gastroenterologist, at Deer Lodge Medical Center. He served our country as part of the United States Air Force Reserves as part of the sixty-fourth aeromedical evacuation flight at Dobbins Air Force Base from 1982 to 1986. He reached the rank of staff sergeant serving as an aeromedical evacuation technician.

My nurse, Zane Cozby, LPN, served in the United States Army. Sergeant Cozby cared for soldiers as a medic in Rahwa, Iraq. He was the medical NCO for the Warrior Transition Unit at Fort Carson, Colorado. I value his knowledge base, experience, and outstanding service to our patients at Deer Lodge Medical Center. We banter over which service is better, Army or Navy, especially when we serve our veteran patients in our rural community. Zane Cozby served the city of Deer Lodge, Montana, as mayor for five years, an interesting fact that caught my attention upon my arrival to Deer Lodge Medical Center. He keeps us all laughing with his hilarious sense of humor. Our patients love him. I am looking forward to working with our caring team for many years to come. Four years have flown by already!

Zane Cozby, active-duty Army medic. Shared on Facebook by Jodi Cozby.

I have been friends with Ellen Rannestad and Steve Ballasch for thirty-seven years and counting along with Ellen's sister, Inger Kantzios. Sergeant Steve Ballasch served at Wright Patterson Air Force Base Medical Center Dental Clinic in Ohio from 1971 to 1974. He recommends serving in the military and taking advantage of the benefits that come from serving. Steve took flying lessons and earned his pilot's license. His most frightening experience while flying occurred when another pilot put the airplane into a spin. Steve earned a bachelor of science degree through the GI Bill benefit. Ellen's father, Andreas Rannestad, born in 1929 in Flel, Norway, met his wife, Ruth E. Hyre Rannestad, at Scott Air Force Base in Illinois. Andreas, a high-ranking Norwegian Air Force engineer with a PhD degree from John Hopkins University, served the government in different capacities, including research, electronic warfare, and scientific affairs to name a few. Ruth, a radio technician, served our country as one of very few women who served at that time. Andreas and Ruth Rannestad had three children, Ellen, Inger, and Susan, who all have dual citizenship in Norway and the United States of America.

Writing *Serving Heroes* proved to be a labor of love. I spent endless hours exploring boxes and totes filled with precious memories of the veterans I served during my career at the VA. Three moves to three different states complicated the search for memorabilia. Additionally, three different computers stored memories and photographs. Technology certainly changed since the time I began my VA career in 2002. I searched through CDs, DVDs, videotapes, flash drives, SanDisk storage devices of various sizes, photo albums, notebooks, and more. I sought permission from veterans and their families by endlessly researching records I kept and, of course, through Google. This is the finished product, a memoir of my life as a doctor working at the VA with a special population of patients, veterans.

I want to thank my husband, Mark, for assisting me by pulling down totes in the search for veteran information and memories. He pulled down the same totes more than once from storage when I was looking for that last little thing I could not go without and include in *Serving Heroes*.

Thank you to Valerie Street Kinney for finding the Honor Flight CAK programs I failed to locate in my tote searches. I know I have them somewhere! I never throw anything out that has to do with veterans.

Thank you to all of the veterans and their families for allowing me to include those veterans who were special in my life as a VA physician. I apologize to those veterans I failed to include, along with their families. I would be happy to publish an addendum to *Serving Heroes* with any new information I receive. I pray those of you who read this book are blessed by it. I wrote the book to honor the veterans and their service to the United States of America. May we keep serving God as our focus and loving others as Jesus Christ commanded us prior to His death, burial, and resurrection. To God be the glory!

ACRONYMS

A1C	Airman First Class
AL	American Legion
ALS	amyotrophic lateral sclerosis (Lou Gehrig's disease)
ASW	anti-submarine warfare
AWACS	airborne warning and control system
CAK	Akron Canton Airport
CBOC	Community Based Outpatient Clinic
CEB	Clinical Executive Board
DAV	Disabled American Veterans
DDS	doctor of dental surgery
DMZ	demilitarized zone
DVA	Department of Veterans Affairs
DO	doctor of osteopathic medicine
ERO	equal rights organization
ODS	Officer Development School
OIG	Office of Inspector General
OSI	opioid safety initiative
GDO	Grievance Division Office
GMO	general medical officer
HFCAK	Honor Flight Akron Canton
HOF	Hall of Fame

HPSP	Health Professional Scholarship Program
IOB	Ignorant Oversight Body
LBB	Legal Battle Board
LSD	landing ship dock
LSM	landing ship medium, landing craft mechanized
LST	landing ship tank
MBA	master of business administration
MCRD	Marine Corps Recruit Depot
MRE	meal ready to eat
NCO	rank of sergeant in the Army
NTC	naval training center
OIS	Officer Indoctrination School
PSB	Professional Standards Board
RV	recreational vehicle
USN	United States Navy
USNR	United States Naval Reserve
VA	Veterans Administration
VFW	Veterans of Foreign Wars
VHA	Veterans Health Administration
VSC	Veteran Service Commission
VVMF	Vietnam Veterans Memorial Fund
WPEA	Whistleblower Protection Enhancement Act of 2012
WWII	World War II

ABOUT THE AUTHOR

Dr. Lori Drumm (Dr. B. Sky) retired from the Department of Veterans Affairs in 2017 and joined the medical team at Deer Lodge Medical Center in Montana. Following service to her country as a general medical officer at Naval Submarine Base New London, she soon chose to serve veterans as a VA primary care physician in Ohio, primary and specialty care service line director in Iowa, and associate chief of staff for primary care and opioid safety initiative champion in Indiana.

Dr. Drumm developed a passion to serve veterans. Her significant accomplishments included partnering with Pegasus Farm to develop the Veterans Salute! program for veterans as part of the therapeutic horseback riding and driving program, traveling with veterans to see their memorials in Washington, DC, as part of the CAK Honor Flight team, riding on the VA float with other veterans in many Pro Football Hall of Fame parades, and attending many other veteran-honoring events. Dr. Drumm earned a master of business administration in health care and graduated from Leadership VA (a national government leadership development program) to support clinical staff in the provision of the best (health) care anywhere in a leadership role. Most importantly, this physician chose to serve veterans, their families, and employees of the VA to bring glory and honor to God.

Dr. Lori Drumm previously published two books with Christian Faith Publishing titled *Oh, the Things They Like to Hide* and *Slaying the Giant, Uncovering the Things They Like to Hide* under the author name, Dr. B. Sky. She lives with her loving and supportive husband in Gold Creek, Montana, enjoying the outdoors fly-fishing, four-wheeling, and snowmobiling.

Ingram Content Group UK Ltd.
Milton Keynes UK
UKHW020746160323
418601UK00011B/233